9.99

This book is due for return on or before the last date shown
above: it may, subject to the book not being reserved by
another reader, be renewed by personal application, post, or
telephone, quoting this date and details of the book.

HAMPSHIRE COUNTY COUNCIL
County Library

 100%
recycled paper

 8/02

FINANCIAL TIMES
Prentice Hall

In an increasingly competitive world, we believe
it's quality of thinking that will give you the edge –
an idea that opens new doors, a technique that solves
a problem, or an insight that simply makes sense of it all.
The more you know, the smarter and faster you can go.

That's why we work with the best minds in business
and finance to bring cutting-edge thinking and best
learning practice to a global market.

Under a range of leading imprints, including *Financial Times
Prentice Hall*, we create world-class print publications and
electronic products bringing our readers knowledge,
skills and understanding which can be applied whether studying
or at work.

To find out more about our business publications, or tell us
about the books you'd like to find, you can visit us at
www.business-minds.com

For other Pearson Education publications, visit
www.pearsoned-ema.com

Pearson
Education

Diary of an Internet Trader

*Practical insights
in investment wisdom*

A l p e s h   B .   P a t e l

FINANCIAL TIMES
Prentice Hall

London   New York   Toronto   Sydney   Tokyo   Singapore   Hong Kong
Cape Town   New Delhi   Madrid   Paris   Amsterdam   Munich   Milan   Stockholm

PEARSON EDUCATION LIMITED

Head Office:
Edinburgh Gate
Harlow CM20 2JE
Tel: +44 (0)1279 623623
Fax: +44 (0)1279 431059

London Office:
128 Long Acre
London WC2E 9AN
Tel: +44 (0)20 7447 2000
Fax: +44 (0)20 7240 5771

Website: www.financialminds.com
www.educationminds.com

First published in Great Britain in 2002

© Tradermind Ltd 2002

The right of Alpesh B. Patel to be identified as Author of this Work has been asserted by him in accordance with the Copyright, Designs and Patents Act 1988.

ISBN: 0 273 65632 5

British Library Cataloguing in Publication Data
A CIP catalogue record for this book can be obtained from the British Library.

10 9 8 7 6 5 4 3 2 1

Designed by Designdeluxe, Bath
Typeset by Northern Phototypesetting Co. Ltd, Bolton
Printed and bound in Great Britain by Bookcraft, Midsomer Norton

The Publishers' policy is to use paper manufactured from sustainable forests.

To my forefathers
for a proud heritage

When I read the Bhagavad Gita and reflect about how God created this universe everything else seems so superfluous. Albert Einstein

I am convinced that everything has come down to us from the banks of the Ganges – astronomy, astrology, metempsychosis. Voltaire

India was China's teacher in religion and imaginative literature, and the world's teacher in trigonometry, quadratic equations, grammar, phonetics, Arabian Nights, animal fables, chess, as well as in philosophy, and that she inspired Boccaccio, Goethe, Herder, Schopenhauer, Emerson, and probably also old Aesop. Lin Yutang, Chinese scholar and author of the book, *The Wisdom of China and India*

Access to the Vedas is the greatest privilege this century may claim over all previous centuries. The general notions about human understanding ... which are illustrated by discoveries in atomic physics are not in the nature of things wholly unfamiliar, wholly unheard of or new. Even in our own culture they have a history, and in Buddhist and Hindu thought a more considerable and central place. What we shall find [in modern physics] is an exemplification, an encouragement, and a refinement of old wisdom. J. Robert Oppenheimer, (1904–1967), theoretical physicist and the Supervising Scientist for the Manhattan Project, the developer of the atomic bomb

The land where books were first written and from where wisdom and knowledge sprang is India. The Fourth Caliph, Ali bin Abi Talib (656–661 AD)

The Hindus are indisputably entitled to rank among the most ancient of existing nations, as well as among those most early and most rapidly civilized ... where yet the Pyramids looked down upon the Valley of the Nile... when Greece and Italy, those cradles of modern civilization, housed only the tenants of the wilderness, India was the seat of wealth and grandeur. Thorton, *History of British India*

The genius of Hinduism, and the very reason of its survival for so long, was that it does not stand up and fight. Mark Tully, former BBC correspondent in India

It is already becoming clear that a chapter which had a Western beginning will have to have an Indian ending if it is not to end in self-destruction of the human race. At this supremely dangerous moment in human history , the only way of salvation is the ancient Hindu way. Here we have the attitude and spirit that can make it possible for the human race to grow together in to a single family. Dr Arnold Joseph Toynbee (1889–1975), British historian

About the author

Alpesh B. Patel
LLB; MA (Oxon); AKC;
Visiting Fellow Corpus Christi
College, Oxford (2001–2),
Barrister-at-Law

Trading

Described by Channel 4 as the UK's best known internet trader, Alpesh started programming computers in BASIC at the age of 10 and buying stocks 18 years ago at the age of 12 (although he seems normal nowadays), moving on from privatization stocks to penny shares. He left a legal career to trade full time.

Today he concentrates on US and UK stocks as well as futures and options trading, making extensive use of the internet for research since he was a Congressional Intern in 1994 and combining this with his own technical analysis systems. On Channel 4's latest *Show Me The Money* series he was number 1 of 45 expert stock pickers.

TV, radio and print

Alpesh writes the *Diary of an Internet Trader* for the weekend **Financial Times** and for **Bloomberg TV** he appears weekly in *Bloomberg Money on the Net*.

Books

Alpesh is the author of *Internet Trading Course, Pocket Guide to Trading Online, Net Trading, Trading Online* and *The Mind of a Trader* (all published by Pearson Education). His books have been translated into Spanish, German, French, Chinese and Polish. *Trading Online* was the number one best-selling investment book on Amazon UK, and reached number two on the overall bestseller list.

Lectures

Alpesh regularly speaks on trading psychology, online trading and technical analysis around the world from Guatemala to Spain to Beijing.

Contents

Picking brokers 73

Portfolio and risk management 93

Active trading 129

Foreign trading 167

Finale 199

Acknowledgements

It would be a mistake to think that, because this is one of several books I have had published by Pearson Education, acknowledgements are owed any the less than for the first book.

I remain grateful as always to Jonathan Agbenyega, who seized the idea and, like all the members of the Pearson team, remained enthusiastic throughout.

As ever, I am sure in the eyes of reader I will receive all credit for the hard work of Penelope Allport, Susan G. R. Williams, and the wonderful, energetic team at Pearson.

But most of all I am grateful because each book is a joy to my parents, and an ambition realized by me.

Alpesh B. Patel
2002

Introduction

Why you need to read this book

Why are some people richer than others? They could both have the same IQ and the same money to start with, the same jobs paying equal salaries; each working as hard as the other and paying the same household expenses. But one of them will end up wealthier. How?

The answer lies in the differing knowledge each has about finances. As JP Morgan recognized: 'Private information is the source of virtually all great wealth.'

The purpose of this book is to disseminate some of that private information – what the rich know and the rest do not. Its findings have been good enough to be published in the *Financial Times* and read worldwide by millions of readers, in the form of my column.

Why do I need to worry about trading online, if I am just going to buy and hold for the long term?

The reason so many people trade online is precisely because buy and hold takes so long to give you any returns at all. Just see the diagram on page xiv.

S&P Composite 1966–1980

140
120
100
80
60
40
20

1/66   10/67   7/69   4/71   1/73   10/74   7/76   4/78   1/80

This 14-year bear market includes the
crash of 1973–74

Adjusted for inflation, the S&P 500 did not
return to its 1966 peak until 1991

Why you need to trade online

Consider the important calculations any sensible investor needs to do before investing. Do you know how to calculate the effect on your portfolio of a 10 per cent market shock? Do you even know why you need to know this? Do you know what type of stocks are most likely to give you growth without volatility?

What if I told you the answer is easy to calculate in seconds online, but with pen and paper would take months. And do you know what the likely reaction of your portfolio will be six months later – the answer is important because otherwise the next time the market dumps 10 per cent how else do you know to sell or hold on?

Not only does this book tell you where to look, but it also tells you why and what the rich online investors know.

What the rich know

So what do rich investors know? Well, here's a summary:

- They know how important it is to have an investment style suited to their needs and goals, and they know how to find it.
- They know how to look for investment opportunity clues on online news stories.
- They know when to switch to short-term investments and when to have long-term ones.
- They know how to save precious time by going straight to the most valuable online sites that do the hard work for you.
- They know which financial securities to trade, not just equities, but also new innovations which give them a head-start advantage.
- They know what *not* to do in selecting a broker and in picking stocks.

This book takes you through all these findings and advice.

Alpesh B. Patel

Picking stocks

What are the different trading styles and which is best for me?

Volatility: How do I buy in on the ground floor and get out at the top?

What do you do if your stock portfolio jumps from $30,000 to $500,000 in five months on over-exuberance, but then falls back to $30,000 three months later, perhaps on under-exuberance? How do you ensure you get in for the upside and get out before the downside?

> How do you ensure you get in for the upside and get out before the downside?

Having a trading style is one way of avoiding the gut-wrenching rollercoaster pain in the financial theme park. A trading style protects profits and avoids losses as the market falls. By adopting a style and understanding what it entails, you develop discipline, avoid confusion and gain fast relief from trading nausea.

Which are the major trading styles used by market professionals?

Here we go…

Momentum

These investors look at the stock price to see whether it is rising and at a rate stronger than its peers. They also look to see whether earnings are exceeding expectations and look for broker upgrades. The traders in this group tend to be short term as they exit as soon as momentum decreases. A momentum trader may have an exit rule such as 'sell half the holding if the stock falls 10 per cent from its most recent high and sell the rest if it falls 15 per cent off its most recent high price'.

Who is this style best suited to?   The style is best suited to those who have the time to monitor the markets and are comfortable with a shorter-term outlook.

Some sites?   Sites providing news about broker updates and earnings estimates include those with AFX news and RNS wires – RNS stands for regulatory news service; it will be bland, basic news, with no interpretation. AFX are news articles from the associated financial press and are therefore opinionated, though the opinion may not be adequate. Most online brokers such as E*Trade (**www.etrade.com**) and Schwab (**www.eschwab.com**) provide this type of news. Price charts are available on the free interactive charting tool from Big Charts (**www.bigcharts.com**) and **eCharts.com**.

Aggressive growth

These investors are often looking for new companies which are growing very quickly. Such companies often have no earnings as they are in the early stages of growth, and tend to have limited trading history, so can be high risk. These investors would have bought QXL.com, ARM or BATM soon after those stocks came on the market. Aggressive growth investors may calculate they could lose at most their initial investment but make many more times that and therefore find the risk-reward ratio attractive.

> Aggressive growth investors may calculate they could lose at most their initial investment but make many more times that and therefore find the risk-reward ratio attractive.

What sort of trader do I have to be to go aggressive? Aggressive growth traders tend to be short term, exiting as growth prospects plateau and moving onto the next aggressive growth stock. Many are found hunting for internet and technology stocks before or shortly after initial public offering (IPO). I don't recommend this strategy to those who are not willing to potentially lose substantial sums in short periods of time in the search for potentially equally substantial gains.

Sites? Sites of particular interest to this breed include **www.eo.com**, **www.issuedirect.com**, **www.newissuesipo.com** and **ipo.com**.

Core growth

These investors will stick to large blue chip stocks that have been the best performers on the Nasdaq, Dow Jones, FTSE 100, etc. in terms of revenue and earnings growth. They are willing to pay the extra in higher valuations that such stocks often carry. Stocks like AstraZeneca, Cisco Systems, GE, GlaxoWellcome and BP Amoco would feature in their portfolios.

Where do I look? Fundamental stock data such as earnings and valuation data is available for such investors from the following excellent sources: Hoovers (**www.hoovers.co.uk**), Hemscott (**www.hemscott.net**), Wright Research Centre (**http://profiles.wisi.com**) and the excellent **www.quicken.com**.

Core value

These traders look for historically low or below sector or industry average price-to-earnings, price-to-book and price-to-sales ratios. The stocks are typically below market average profitability, but the investor expects a turnaround and buys and holds until that occurs and the market revalues the stocks. Energy and financial stocks tend to be favoured by these investors.

Websites for the core value trader are the same as for the core growth investor.

Deep value

These traders are a more aggressive version of core value investing. They seek extremely low valuations and go for especially unfavoured sectors and stocks. They are sometimes called 'contrarians' and often seek drastic corporate changes such as takeovers, management buy outs or sale of assets.

Growth

These traders are more aggressive than core growth traders but less so than aggressive growth traders. They will avoid relatively overvalued stocks even if they are blue chip in the search for stocks likely to grow better than average. They may look towards relatively undervalued medium-cap stocks with better than sector average revenue growth rates.

Sites? The medium to longer-term traders will find the news sites and fundamental data sites mentioned above the most useful.

Growth at a reasonable price (GARP)

These investors are looking for presently undervalued stocks with the potential to outgrow the market. This strategy is more conservative than a growth strategy and tends to be medium to longer term in outlook. Sites providing company financial data, especially valuation data mentioned above, are the most useful to this type of online trader.

They would have steered clear of most internet stocks since these were either loss-making or overvalued on traditional valuation measures such as price-earnings (P/E) ratios.

How do I choose the best trading style?

Trading style selection should be based on your trading experience, your aversion to risk and the sums of money you are willing to risk, and your personality. For instance, until a couple of years ago I was too impatient for 'buy and hold' strategies, preferring the quick performance feedback that comes from momentum trading. Equally, I am not comfortable with aggressive growth investing as I do not find the win-loss ratios attractive. Presently, I have a momentum-based portfolio and a core growth portfolio.

Which type of traders have the best performance record?

If you are comfortable with different styles then, unlike a fund manager, you could take advantage of the freedom you have to switch styles.

For the past few years momentum traders have outperformed value investors. However, that may now be changing. If you are comfortable with different styles then, unlike a fund manager, you could take advantage of the freedom you have to switch styles.

The above classification is not exhaustive and you should also remember that the likely returns from different trading styles vary according to market conditions.

9

WHAT ARE THE DIFFERENT TRADING STYLES AND WHICH IS BEST FOR ME?

Figure 1.1 The erratic performances of fund managers suggest picking the right fund is more an accident than a skill

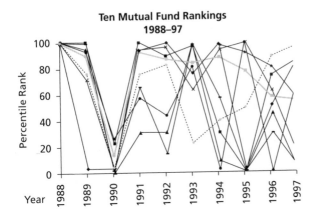

Ten Mutual Fund Rankings 1988–97

———▲——— MSCI Emerging Market Index
———■——— MSCI Emerging Mkt. Mid, Latin American Index
———▲——— MSCI AC Far East ex Japan Index
———∗——— Kaufman
———✕——— SunAmerica Small Growth Co A
——————— Columbia Special
———◆——— Parnassus
———●——— American Cent-Ben Tar Mat 2015
            Chase Vista Grow & Inc. A
······◦····· Ariel Growth

How do I use online trading stock news to my advantage?

There is so much online trading share news – how do I use it?

News is important. It allows us to get a feel for why the market is moving, then why a sector may be moving, and downwards onto an industry then into a stock (see Fig 2.1). News has many functions for the trader.

Figure 2.1 Layers of news

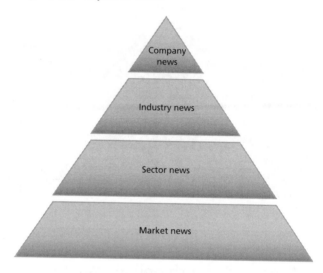

What types of focus should I give and what questions should I be asking?

Look at Table 2.1. There is a lot of information on the web and you have little time. Therefore you need to know where to go to get the knowledge you require and how to use it once you have it.

At the outset of your trading you must have a general idea of what parts of the economy are doing well. Your aim as an online trader is to invest in those projects that will present you with the highest possible return relative to the plethora of other available investment projects, over a given period of time.

Table 2.1 Types of news and their uses for the online trader

Type of news	Uses
Market news	■ Is the market in trouble? ■ Is there much negative news that will stop stocks soaring? ■ Are there economic problems in the economy, such as high inflation, low growth, strikes, political uncertainty, low productivity, all of which will impact stock price rises?
Sector	■ Which sectors are rising and which are falling? ■ Is there sector rotation, i.e. some sectors accelerate while others fall? ■ Is there growth in certain sectors, e.g. technology, and trouble with others, e.g. consumer goods?
Industry	■ More specifically, which industries in a sector are enjoying good growth? ■ Is there news about positive telecoms development or negative tobacco issues?
Company	■ Is the company generating a sound, positive stream of news? ■ Or is it warning of earnings problems? Good news flows should be reflected in strong upward price moves. How is the price faring?

But there are so many areas to invest in

Therefore you need to have a starting point, otherwise you will be swamped. A good starting point is to ask general questions about the markets and stocks and then proceed to answer those questions. As you work your way through the chapter, answer the following questions:

- Which markets am I interested in?
- Is the general economy doing well?
- Which sectors am I interested in?
- Is the US telecoms sector (or other sector you may be interested in) suffering?
- Which telecoms stocks have been popular?

All this questioning – what purpose does it serve?

Questioning is the first stage of analysis. It helps to focus your thoughts so that you can create an efficient plan of action. But it's not enough to ask questions. Here is where the general market news comes in. Financial and market news is crucial because it answers your queries and encourages further questioning.

And, of course, if you wish to trade on the market index, e.g. the FTSE 100 or the Nasdaq, rather than any particular company, general market news is directly important.

What types of news articles should I look at?

Table 2.2 Different news styles

Type of news	What it provides	How to use it
Newswire (also called market pulse) (Fig 2.2)	A quick-fire summary of news items. Limited analysis. Mainly just describes what has happened. We have to do most of our own analysis.	Can give us advance warning of impending price moves. Most useful to short-term active trader because of its likely impact on prices in the short term.
Column (commentary) (Fig 2.3)	A regular writer offers a daily or weekly piece on a particular issue such as telecoms stocks or emerging market stocks.	The columnist is usually taking the recent newswires and adding a bit more analysis and opinion to them – explaining their significance to us. They give us a clearer picture of which stocks we should investigate further.

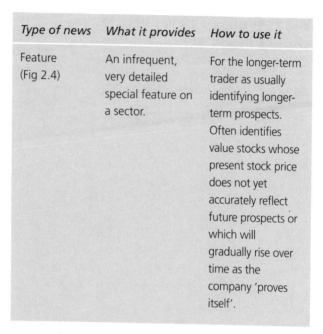

Type of news	What it provides	How to use it
Feature (Fig 2.4)	An infrequent, very detailed special feature on a sector.	For the longer-term trader as usually identifying longer-term prospects. Often identifies value stocks whose present stock price does not yet accurately reflect future prospects or which will gradually rise over time as the company 'proves itself'.

Figure 2.2 Newswire

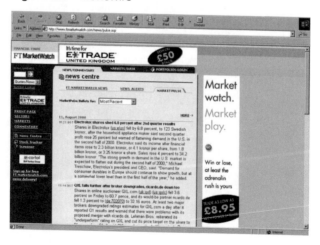

Figure 2.3 Column

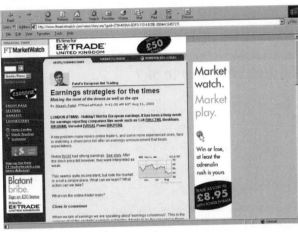

Figure 2.4 Special feature

All news is not the same, and each type of news has different uses for the trader. We need to appreciate the different types of news and how to use them – see Table 2.2.

Where should I look?

Here are some of the best news sites. The sites listed in the next section on researching individual companies will also be useful for general news.

411 Stocks ***

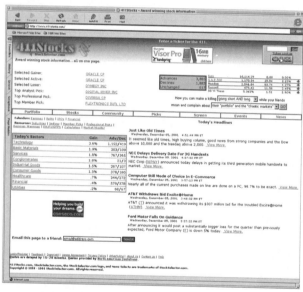

www.411stock.com

This is a simple megasite for finding information about a stock. Provides price data, news, discussion groups, charting, fundamental data and income statements. A lot of information in one place.

Bloomberg ***

www.bloomberg.com

An abundance of news and commentary in a no-nonsense format. Excellent reporting, sharp presentation and speed for top-notch coverage of industry, markets, hi-tech stocks and the global economy. The site is cleanly designed. Valuable information delivered well.

CBS MarketWatch ***

www.cbs.marketwatch.com

Front page packs essential breaking stories on the market and companies. The information is well organized and easy to navigate, with keyword searches. Links in articles are well thought out. Free tools include company research, charts and delayed quotes.

CNNfn ***

www.cnnfn.com

With its reporters worldwide the site is able to break news and offer a very fast newswire service. Its writers also do more in-depth thoughtful, analytical pieces which we as traders can use too.

The Financial Times **

www.ft.com

The reliable pink pages online has full access to its leading companies and markets news. It also has a searchable archive and you can get news e-mailed to you.

Also see FTMarketWatch at **www.ftmarketwatch.com** – decent market coverage and analysis. Offers an assortment of model portfolios. Well-written articles. The design is uncluttered.

LatinFocus ***

www.latin-focus.com

Sharp site for investors in select Central and South American countries. Pull-up detailed economic profiles packed with data. An excellent place for initial research.

Money.net ***

www.moneynet.net

Free streaming real-time quotes. Recently added improved market news and message boards. Very valuable.

MSNBC **

www.msnbc.com

Bill Gates foray into all things financial. Credible because it is linked with NBC. Very user friendly.

Reuters Moneynet **

www.moneynet.com

Market commentary is very good. Breaking news. Category news and companies prominent in the news today will all be very helpful to get you started. However, little visual variety makes it a bit monotonous.

Wall Street Journal **

www.wsj.com

The main problem with this site is the annoying registration aspect. Other than that the news content is best for thoughtful pieces, not necessarily the newswire aspects.

WorldlyInvestor ***

www.worldlyinvestor.com

An excellent collection of columns and in-depth features from industry practitioners, which means they are especially insightful and helpful to the trader. The site is well organized so you can focus on the sectors in which you are most interested.

I want to see which sectors the websites are picking up on. Are there any sectors they think are particularly interesting?

Well, I would click on the CBS MarketWatch site which always has useful, insightful commentary – the type that knows what is really happening in the markets and is written for traders to profit from (Fig 2.5).

Figure 2.5 CBS MarketWatch headlines

The headline which catches my attention is 'Tobacco gets a buzz' – clearly, there has been some positive news surrounding tobacco issues and I may want to investigate this sector further. So I read on (Fig 2.6).

Figure 2.6 The news gets more detailed

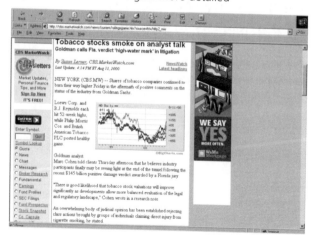

EXERCISES – YOU HAVE A GO

Visit four of the sites listed above and scan for two
major economy or sector stories that suggest further investigation may lead to good stocks to
research.

Remember as you do this:

- the clue is in the headlines;
- it should not take time – the headlines should
  jump out at you;
- after the headline see which subtitle looks the
  most promising;
- print out the story for later cross-reference to
  assist in your research and to keep in a folder so
  that it can help with your trade planning (more
  about this later) if you decide to buy the stock.

Jot down your findings here:

Site:	Headline:	Potential stocks to investigate:
____	____	____
____	____	____
____	____	____
____	____	____

Should I listen to the commentary?

But how do you know whether you should listen to that one commentator on that one site? Easy:

1. Is it a well-respected site such as the ones I have listed here? If it is not listed above, is it one whose brand you have come across before?

2. Scan a few other sites. Do any of them pick up a similar theme, e.g. tobacco stocks likely to rally?

3. Make a note of the stock names and the reasons the site gives, then use them later when you do your own research and confirm for yourself whether you agree these stocks are a good buy or a goodbye. A good trader doesn't take anyone's word for it but his own.

But surely if the story is in the headlines the stock price will already have jumped?

This can sometimes be true for very immediate price moves, but if you are a longer-term holder it need not be a problem. We are looking for the types of news stories that suggest the price has yet to move up, are forward looking, for instance something headed:

Telecoms undervalued

Pharmaceuticals still further to ride

Housebuilders may end slide

I have heard about a company and am interested in it as a potential investment – how do I gauge whether I should invest into this company?

The news is a starting point, but it's time for you to decide whether the company looks good enough for *you*.

What kind of things would I want to know about a potential investment?

Here are a few suggestions:

- What exactly is their business and how big is it?
- Any major items of recent news about the company.
- How much profit analysts think it will make in the future; the firm's business strategy.
- What other investors have thought of it.
- How its share price has performed in the last few years.
- How their accounts look – how profitable they are and how profitable they can be.

For now let us focus on company-specific news.

What procedures should I follow?

To find out news about a specific company using any of the excellent sites mentioned above is relatively easy as they all follow a similar format.

Ticker box

The first thing you need is the company's ticker symbol. The symbol lookup link under the ticker box will help you find the ticker symbol for your stock. You then enter that into any appropriate box – see Figs 2.7 and 2.8. You will then be taken to more detailed information about the stock, which usually includes the most recent news.

Figure 2.7 Symbol lookup link and ticker box symbol

Figure 2.8 Symbol lookup box for searching company tickers

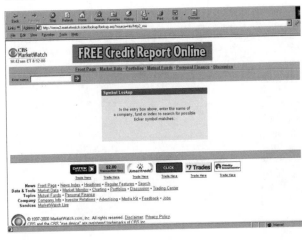

Story

Often, however, whenever a company is mentioned in a story the company name is underlined, meaning if you click on it you will be taken to more information about the company, including news (see Fig 2.9). Some sites allow you to search for news but the same principle applies (Fig 2.10). Fig 2.11 shows how CBS MarketWatch presents the news.

Figure 2.9 Clicking on highlighted stock names takes you to more information about those companies, including news

Figure 2.10 News search facility – this is not available on most sites, but **Ft.com** and **Moneynet.com** have good search facilities

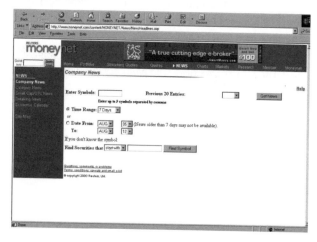

Figure 2.11 All the news from Microsoft

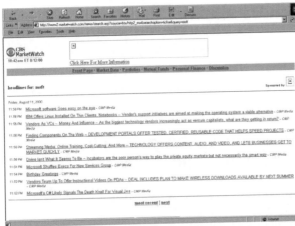

EXERCISES

1. Find the ticker symbols for the following four stocks:

   ■ Cisco (US).
   ■ Sun Microsystems (US).
   ■ Atlantic Telecom (UK).
   ■ France Telecom (French).

2. For each of these companies find both the latest and historical news using one of the websites mentioned above.

What about news about non-US stocks?

Simply go to a site that caters for this type of news. For example, FTMarketWatch will give you stock symbols and news for UK and European companies as well as US ones.

What should I be looking for in a company newsflow?

Positive news items about the company include:

- winning new orders;
- increasing orders;
- entry into new sectors;
- new product developments;
- good strategic alliances;
- accelerations in the current business model.

We also want to know what the analysts are forecasting for upcoming profits. This is worth knowing because analysts receive regular private briefings from the company on how things are going and so are usually on the mark with their estimates.

Finding out what other investors have thought of the company through 'chat rooms' and 'share picks' is interesting since you can gauge other people's opinion. If there is some aspect of the company you are wondering about or cannot understand, other people's opinions will be helpful. However, there are various warnings that are stamped on these sorts of prescriptions, so beware.

Remember: an investor's opinion is just one estimation, one outlook, not the last word.

How do I scan newsflow?

Since there are many news items and we want to be as efficient as possible so that we can make our money and actually have time to spend it instead of sitting in front of the computer all the time, we need to know how to scan these news headlines.

The general rule is that news companies try to tell as much as possible in the headline. Consequently I tend to focus on those headlines which common sense tells me are likely to include some of the information I am looking for. In the example below I have highlighted the ones I consider in that category out of a series for Sun Microsystems. However, I may also examine some of the others if I think I need more information about a stock.

The following newsflow for Sun Microsystems shows some headlines which merit further investigation.

headlines for: sunw

Friday, August 11, 2000

11:56 PM	Startup Axient Bets On Private Fiber Network — WITH A 60-CITY NETWORK, AXIENT GETS DEAL FROM NBC TO DELIVER BROADBAND OLYMPIC COVERAGE – *CMP Media*
11:56 PM	Vendors As VCs — Money And Influence — As the biggest technology vendors increasingly act as venture capitalists, what are they getting in return? – *CMP Media*

11:56 PM	Finding Components On The Web — DEVELOPMENT PORTALS OFFER TESTED, CERTIFIED, REUSABLE CODE THAT HELPS SPEED PROJECTS – *CMP Media*
11:52 PM	The New Developer Portals — BUYING, SELLING, AND BUILDING COMPONENTS ON THE WEB SPEEDS COMPANIES' TIME TO MARKET – *CMP Media*
11:51 PM	Vendors Partner With Venture Capitalists To Fund Startups – *CMP Media*
11:50 PM	The Two Faces Of E-Biz Management – *CMP Media*
11:50 PM	**Sun teams with vignette – *CMP Media***
11:50 PM	Stealing Java's Thunder — Microsoft's upcoming Visual Studio.net offers an integrated development interface, a new programming language, and programming shortcuts that should result in more-efficient Web development. A secondary, unstated aim is to slow Java's progress – *CMP Media*
11:39 PM	AMD, Intel draw 64-bit battle lines – *CMP Media*
11:37 PM	XML GAINS MOMENTUM — ebXML emerging as EDI alternative for B2B transactions – *CMP Media*
6:05 PM	GSA Awards FirstGov Contract to GRC International – *PRNewswire*

4:14 PM	WRAP: Dell shares fall 11% on concerns about future sales growth (Update 1) – *Futures World News Select*
3:46 PM	LinuxWorld Conference & Expo Exhibitor Profiles A to Z; Conference and Expo to Start Next Week in San Jose, Calif. – *BusinessWire*
2:47 PM	Stock picks of the week: EMC, Pfizer, Sun, Johnson & Johnson and H-P – *Deborah Adamson* CBS MarketWatch.com
12:54 PM	First Ecom.com Inc. Announces Second Quarter Financial Results – *BusinessWire*
11:02 AM	Robinson-Humphrey Analyst Interviews On RadioWallStreet.com – *BusinessWire*
9:45 AM	Planet City Software Teams With CRD Capital – *PRNewswire*

Thursday, August 10, 2000

11:01 PM	Sun, Microsoft Java Battle Delayed – *Unknown (cmtx-pc)*
8:23 PM	James J. Whitney Named Forsythe Solutions Group's E-Business Solutions Technologist – *BusinessWire*
8:13 PM	PVI, Sportvision, Inc. Named Winners Success Story Receives Recognition from Sun Microsystems, Computerworld Competition – *PRNewswire*

EXERCISE

Find and then highlight the most important news items for the Indian technology company Satyam which is listed in the US under ticker code SIFY.

- Did you learn anything about US corporate investment in India?
- Did you find out the names of major US companies investing in India?
- Did you discover Indian economic conditions?
- Has Satyam entered into recent alliances?
- What other interesting stock moving news was there for the stock?

Can you give a quick summary of key terms?

Technical analysis – methods used to forecast future prices using the price data alone (for example by plotting it as a chart and noting direction) or using the price as an input in mathematical formulae and plotting the results. Contrast this with fundamental analysis.

Fundamental analysis – forecasting prices by using economic or accounting data. For example one might base a decision to buy a stock on its yield.

Market capitalization – this is the product of the number of shares outstanding and the current price.

Director dealings – whether the directors have been buying or selling shares in their company.

Should I also look using a search engine?

Of course. The internet is a huge expanse of information and if you want to navigate it and find the information you want, you will have to search. A search engine is simply a site that 'searches' other sites depending on keywords entered by a user. Search engines are therefore of general use, not just for the online trader.

How should I search?

Simple: type in the keyword and press enter. If you want to be technical, most search engines will have options which allow you to specify whether the engine is to provide results that contain the keywords as a phrase or any one of the keywords.

■ Since pages on the internet change quickly, a search engine is unlikely to be up to the minute and some results may be out of date.

■ Just because an engine does not find a site does not mean it does not exist.

■ Because of the different ways search engines work, each will return different results.

■ If you are not satisfied with the results, try a different engine.

■ Results are ranked according to the closeness of the match to your request and not according to the best available site in terms of content.

Which are the top search engine sites?

Use these sites yourself to search for information on specific areas of trading:

■ Altavista   **www.altavista.com**

■ Excite   **www.excite.com**

■ Lycos   **www.lycos.com**

■ Yahoo!   **www.yahoo.com**

SELF-ASSESSMENT

1. Which one of these is not something you would find a useful piece of market news?
    a. Inflation projections.
    b. Last year's inflation figures.
    c. Expected growth rates.
    d. Possible foreign armed conflict.

2. What is sector rotation?

3. What is another name for a newswire service?
   a. Market wire.
   b. Market rotation.
   c. Market pulse.
   d. Market beat.

4. To what type of trader is a newswire most useful?
   a. Active short-term traders.
   b. Medium-term traders.
   c. Long-term traders.

5. Which has the least analysis?
   a. Market pulse.
   b. Column.
   c. Special feature.

6. Does stock price always react to news?

7. Name a site that provides news on non-US securities by allowing you to enter their ticker symbols.

Answers:

1. **b** – because they are backward looking. While they are relevant in shaping this year's expectations, they are too far in the past to have market influence.

2. Where sectors that were not increasing in price start growing as money rotates into them and out of previously leading sectors.

3. Market pulse (used for instance by **FTMarketWatch.com**).

4. Active short-term traders as such news is purely factual and tends to influence the immediate price, although it can often have longer ramifications, depending on how it is interpreted.

5. Market pulse – it tends to be factual reporting, not with opinion.

6. No – that is one reason why trading is so difficult.

7. **www.ftmarketwatch.com**, for example.

Is long-term trading really 'all that and a bag of cash'?

What are long-term online investors to do when markets head for the floor?

Not to fear, there is much to help you keep your nerve through such turbulent times. Consider that since 1950 US investors have experienced more than 29 market corrections (when the market declines by 10 per cent or more) and 11 bear markets (a 20 per cent decline) based on the S&P 500. The average length of these bear markets has merely been around seven months, with an average decline of 28 per cent.

However, based on the same index, the average bull market lasts 47 months, with an increase of 123 per cent – well worth waiting for if you are a buy and hold investor

However, based on the same index, the average bull market lasts 47 months, with an increase of 123 per cent – well worth waiting for if you are a buy and hold investor.

What if I lose my nerve and exit, hoping to re-enter once things appear more bullish?

According to Fidelity, one of the world's largest fund managers, if in 1980 you invested $10,000 tracking the S&P 500, by 2000 your investment would have been worth $185,000. If, however, in an attempt to 'time' your entry and exit you missed the best 1 per cent of days in the past 20 years, you would have had a mere $34,000.

Of course, Fidelity fails to tell us what would happen if in attempting to time the market you missed the worst 1 per cent of days.

What strategies might the buy and hold investor adopt in these difficult conditions to shore up his nerves?

Dollar cost averaging is one way to ensure falling markets are not all bad news.

Huh?

Here the online investor makes periodic purchases regardless of market movements. It reduces your cost per share because you are buying more shares when prices are down and fewer shares when prices are high. For instance, say you intended to buy $12,000 of IBM stock on the first trading day of January 2002. Instead of making the whole investment, you may reason that since you do not know the best time to buy you will cost average and invest $1,000 monthly in the stock instead.

> Cost averaging yields impressive results even if in the short term markets fall as long as in the long term they rise

Such cost averaging yields impressive results even if in the short term markets fall as long as in the long term they rise. The sum of $2,000 invested in the S&P 500 annually since 1975 even on the worst possible day each year (the market high) would turn to more than $500,000 in profits by 2000, according to Micropal, the special fund monitoring and research company.

Any more strategies?

Yep. Another way for buy and hold online investors to reinforce their nerves as the turbulent market dents their portfolios is to remember that stock returns become less volatile over longer periods.

Take the S&P 500 during 1926–1995. Returns over a rolling one-year period fluctuated from +50 per cent to –50 per cent. Over a rolling ten-year period that drops to +20 per cent to –1 per cent. Longer holding periods reduce risk of loss. Of course, the downside is that it reduces spectacular gains, too.

Try **www.hemscott.net** and **bigcharts.com** for free long-term online share charts.

Is the long-term view the best way to go?

Well, of course the best reason for buy and hold investors to hold their nerve is the billionaire investor Warren Buffett. Berkshire Hathaway, his investment company, has produced a 24 per cent growth per share in book value for the past 35 years.

Unfortunately, my impatience prevents me from ever becoming a long-term buy and holder. Even Warren Buffett missed the TMT (technology, media and telecoms stocks) mania gains of 1999. He didn't buy technology stocks because he correctly reasoned that overvalued stocks are not a good long-term buy. However, those who profited from the rise in TMT shares in 1999 and (because of their short-term perspective) exited as the market fell in 2000 will over the two years 1999–2000 have outperformed Buffett. (If you're a tech head, check out **www.herring.com** and **www.interstocks.com**.)

> Even Warren Buffett missed the TMT (technology, media and telecoms stocks) mania gains of 1999.

So it depends then?

The trick for the short-term trader is to be able to maintain that outperformance and not get caught in the slump. And that really does require some nerve.

Figs 3.1, 3.2 and 3.3 make the point that if you are thinking of being a long-term investor, then you really need to be very long term because in the short term portfolio returns are all over the place; only over decades do they rise consistently. Portfolio numbers refer to differing levels of risk, from 10 the lowest to 90 the greatest.

Figure 3.1 Annual returns over 27 years

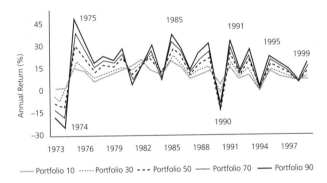

—— Portfolio 10 ······ Portfolio 30 - - - Portfolio 50 —— Portfolio 70 —— Portfolio 90

Figure 3.2 Every 3-year returns over 27 years

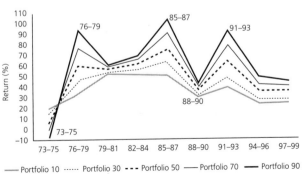

—— Portfolio 10 ······ Portfolio 30 - - - Portfolio 50 —— Portfolio 70 —— Portfolio 90

Figure 3.3 Every 9-year returns over 27 years

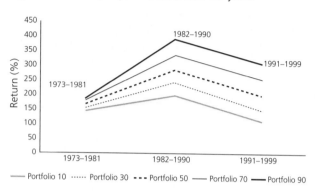

chapter four

What's all this technical analysis and charting about then?

How can I predict which way a stock is going to go?

This question is at the heart of any choice about a stock – all other questions flow from this one. One way of evaluating whether a stock price will rise is to analyze how the price has moved in the past. Technical analysis (or TA to its friends) is a basis for forecasting future prices using (recent) past price data.

So, is there any more to TA?

Technical analysis is a method of determining opportune buying and selling points. It involves methods used to forecast future prices using the price data alone (for example by plotting it as a chart and noting direction) or using the price as an input in mathematical formulae and plotting the results. Contrast this with fundamental analysis, which looks at a company's accounts, reports, etc. in order to evaluate price moves.

Whenever we use TA, or any other form of analysis, we are, in fact, looking for points where there is an increased *probability* of a price move. We look for areas into which it is highly probable that the price will move.

When is TA a better tool than fundamentals?

Well, TA tends to work best over a time frame of a few days to a few months, so it is ideal for short-term to medium-term trading. Many of the indicators and methods of analysis we will examine are trying to determine when traders may have overreacted and therefore have sold too much stock too quickly or vice versa, and therefore afford us the opportunity to enter or exit the market at the best time to maximize profits.

However, TA does not always work. It cannot explain everything in the market, since the market does not behave in a necessarily consistent manner.

What are the basic tools and strategies?

I am not going to go through every single analytic method known to man and beast. I am going to focus on the techniques I use, that are the most popular and that the major institutions use. At the end of this chapter you won't have a PhD in TA, but that doesn't matter – you're going to use TA, not lecture on it.

Let us start from the top. The first thing all technical analysts will do is put up a price chart, of which there are many types.

Bar charts (Fig 4.1) are the most popular way of depicting prices. The extremities of the price high and the low determine the length. The horizontal line on the left of each vertical line represents the opening price, and the horizontal line on the right represents the close.

Figure 4.1   Bar chart

In the Japanese candlestick (Fig 4.2) there is a 'body' and a line (like a wick). The body is a rectangle drawn between the open and close of the day. It is shaded black if the close is lower than the open, and white if the close is above the open. The wick is added to join the high and low of the day. Of course, if there is no price movement after the open, there will be no body or wick, just a horizontal line.

Figure 4.2   Japanese candlestick

There are many more, including the straightforward line chart (Fig 4.3), but you get the point.

Figure 4.3   Line chart

What do I do with these charts? What am I looking for?

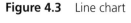

In a word, trends. A trendline simply joins a series of higher lows and lower highs.

Uh?

Look at Fig 4.4. We see the line joining higher and higher lows. Drawing trendlines is an art and you should not look for exact points but a feel of where prices are hitting the approximate narrow area around the line and then moving back up. What trendlines try to represent are areas where there is a relatively increased probability of a price move off the trendline. You would not trade off the trendline, but rather use it as one piece of evidence when determining likely price moves.

Figure 4.4   The trend is your friend

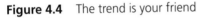

Is there any more to trendlines?

By drawing support and resistance levels we are again trying to determine areas where prices are *probably*, but not *certainly*, going to behave in a particular way (see Fig 4.5). This shows support and resistance levels, the lower line being the support. So for instance, when the price approaches the resistance area, it has greater difficulty getting past that area and you may decide you want to exit your position (if you are holding one) at that point.

Figure 4.5   Support and resistance levels

Like trendlines, support and resistance levels are not set in stone. They are liable to move and can be penetrated intra-day or over a couple of days. They are zones of probable price action.

With trendlines and supports and resistances, the probability of a price move in a particular direction increases the longer the trendline has been in 'force', i.e. not been significantly penetrated. For example, if the price has hit the trendline on five occasions and then moved up, it should do the same the sixth time it hits the trend.

So what is the explanation of price movements along a trendline?

With supports and resistances what we are seeing is a battle between buyers and sellers. For instance, at a resistance level sellers may have decided they will start selling a security at that level because it is overpriced, and buyers are too few to do much about it. So the price has to retreat as selling increases. If buyers increase in number and size at the crucial point then the price may break through with the force of a broken dam, marauding buyers thus pushing the price higher and higher. This is one reason why price often jumps at breakouts with a sharp rise, a gap in price and large volume.

What should I look for?

Look for penetration or breakthrough of the resistance – if there is one it should be followed by a big move. An alternative method of trading is to wait and see if the trendline or support is not broken, and then trade in the direction of the rebound.

What counts as penetration of the trendline?

Given market volatility you could get price piercing a trendline or support or resistance but then closing back above. For this reason, some analysts only draw trendlines and supports based on closing prices, because intra-day prices are too erratic. Others say the price must close for two or three days in the penetration position.

■ When a support or resistance level is broken it tends then to reverse its role and become a resistance level or a support level respectively (see Fig 4.6). This is a common occurrence known as a 'reversal pattern' and the same rules apply as before.

■ After a breakthrough of a support or resistance the price will often 'pull back' to the trendline it has just broken through. You have to be careful of this as you may think the move has just ended, in which case you may exit an otherwise profitable trade prematurely.

What patterns suggest a turning point in the share price – hopefully indicating an up-turn?

Reversal patterns

These are chart patterns which historically have tended to precede a reversal in prices. Again, they are added to our overall evidence of what the price may do, which gives a better idea of whether we should exit a position or enter one.

Head and shoulders strategies

An anatomical pattern this. Take a look at Fig 4.6. It is not always as clear-cut. This is a common pattern on bar charts and fairly reliable. The horizontal line represents the 'neckline' and you always wait for it to be broken for it to be a head and a shoulder position. The pattern can occur on a slope. The position can also occur as a bullish (rising share price) pattern if it appears as an opposite or mirror reflection.

Figure 4.6 Head and shoulders

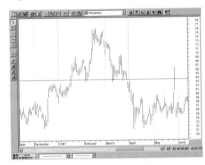

Triangle strategies

Figure 4.7 shows a triangle. For a price reversal on the upside the horizontal line appears above the ascending diagonal line. We are then looking for a breakout of the horizontal line. To trade the pattern you can treat it very much like a breakout pattern from a resistance level. Volume should be decreasing to the apex and then increase on breakout as the marauding purchasing invaders breach the sellers' line of defence. Below is an ascending triangle; the descending triangle is an exact mirror reflection and would represent a price breakout on the downside.

Figure 4.7 Triangle

Saucer strategies

The pattern for this is shown in Fig 4.8. It represents a gradual change in opinion about a stock. Although a saucer is rare, if you can spot them as the price is rising they can be an additional confirmatory indicator of a trend change. There are no price targets for this pattern so exit needs to be determined more by rising percentage stop-losses or exit points determined by other technical methods.

Figure 4.8 Saucer

What patterns suggest that share prices will continue to move in the current direction?

Continuation patterns

These patterns confirm that the current direction of price movement will continue. They can represent a pause in price and so can be used as a good point to step on before the escalator starts moving up again.

Rectangles

The rectangle is simply where the price action moves sideways between a support and resistance level after a rise. It can be thought of as a resting place where buying and selling troops stop to reconsider the price levels.

A strategy for this is to trade it in the same way you would any other breakout of a resistance. Unlike a normal breakout, the fact that price has risen up to the rectangle formation adds to the likelihood of the breakout.

Flag strategies

A flag can appear in an uptrend or downtrend (see Fig 4.9). The flag looks like a rectangle rotated diagonally upwards and is preceded by a downtrend. The flag is where, instead of a sideways move after a downturn, buyers for a while outgun sellers and cause prices to rise, as they believe prices have oversold, but the sellers soon return as price rises. The flag is important only after the bottom of the flag is pierced – so wait for that. If it is not pierced, you simply have a reversal.

Figure 4.9 Flag

Pennant strategy

The pennant shows a rising trend followed by a price move where low boundary lines converge, representing the battle between buyers and sellers. Volume should decrease to the apex and increase on the breakout of the upper boundary. You can treat the breakout of the upper boundary in the same way for trading as we discussed before about trading breakouts generally (see Fig 4.10).

Figure 4.10 Pennant

What general lessons should I note when looking for the above TA patterns?

Before moving on we should make a general point about how the TA tools examined are to be used as part of your overall trading strategy. Remember:

■ Any single tool is not sufficient as the basis of a trading decision.

■ The tools must be used in conjunction, each providing further confrmation or not. Find out which tools are best for you.

■ The TA tools must also be used to precisely time your entry or exit from a position. Timing your entry or exit is critical, since it is not enough to think the price will rise or fall in the next couple of weeks. TA is a fine-tuner.

Is it easier to trade a sector than a stock or a whole index?

Is picking the right sector easier than picking the right stock?

Of course it is. It is easier to predict how a sector will go than a specific stock in a sector. Moreover, volatility either reclaims stock gains or results in downright losses.

What about an index?

Contrast indices and individual stocks with sectors and your chances of a return seem to improve.

So why don't all online traders invest in sectors and not just stocks?

Because until recently it was far easier to buy a stock. But no more. Exchange traded funds (ETFs) are one way to invest in sectors – see **www.morningstar. com**; **www.indesfunds.com/ETFzone.htm** ETFs represent a portfolio of stocks and are available on European sectors, for example, as 'iShares' (www.ishares.net) such as the iBloomberg European Resources. Unfortunately the iShares are available on only a limited number of sectors and all are pan-European. US sectors, by contrast, are well covered by other ETFs called 'holders' **(www.holders.com)**.

You can trade ETFs just like a stock through online brokers such as **www.dljdatek.com, www.ameritrade.com, www.fastrade.co.uk** and **www.fimatex.co.uk**.

How are they different to trusts?

Unlike trusts, you can trade them any time during market hours on real-time prices. And unlike a sector investment trust, such as those listed on **www.moneyextra.com**, you would know exactly the composition of the portfolio of stocks throughout the day.

Does this mean I can trade actively?

Yes, such characteristics make active trading easier too, allowing easy and quick exits should sector sentiment change rapidly.

But how do you anticipate a rising sector?

By examining sector rotation – the movement of cash from some sectors into others. I look for signs of rotation by

63

IS IT EASIER TO TRADE A SECTOR THAN A STOCK OR A WHOLE INDEX?

examining weekly sector gains and losses covering fortnightly and monthly periods. Sectors with consecutive periods of increasing gains are clearly the ones money is entering. Comdirect.co.uk and my own creation, **www.pathburner.com/sectors.asp**, have useful sector charts.

What other ways can I anticipate rotation?

Another way to anticipate sector rotation is to examine their price charts for period-on-period growth on software. Finally, look at newsflow and analysts' reports covered by sites such as **www.digitallook.co.uk** and **www.ftmarketwatch.com**.

How should online traders interpret strong sector growth?

Any sector that rises strongly will evoke two types of reaction from online traders. First, it's gone up so much so soon, it must be ready for profit taking and therefore too late to enter. The opposing view is, what's been working for the past three months is hardly about to stop working without some sector-wide bad news, and so the trend should continue.

So who's right?

I follow the second view: wait for price improvement following newsflow and positive analyst comment, even risking getting in a little bit late, then stay in for the rise until the price (not necessarily poor newsflow) shows weakness by making new, say five or six-day, lows.

Of course, there is a price to pay for picking sectors, surely?

Well, you're not going to get the huge returns a stock can provide. By definition a sector cannot outperform its best performing stock. However, you won't have the kinds of losses you could have with a stock either. In essence, sectors are more forgiving than stocks and that can make them more rewarding, too.

> Sectors are more forgiving than stocks and that can make them more rewarding, too

Inspire me that an online trader really can beat the professionals

And the prize for best fund manager goes to…you – the online investor. In second place is the professional full-time fund manager.

The top 100 online investors on Marketocracy.com not only outperformed 99.8 per cent of all US professional fund managers during the second quarter of 2001, they also outperformed all the main market indices, too.

Surely these online investors are outperforming professionals by taking excessive risks?

Well, Marketocracy.com requires them to abide by strict rules which all online investors should consider.

How?

First, no position can exceed 25 per cent of your total portfolio value. Second, half your portfolio must be comprised of positions under 5 per cent each. Third, you must classify whether your investment style is growth, value or a blend of the two. This last rule ensures an added professionalism and discipline.

Am I outperforming professional fund managers too? How do I measure my online portfolio?

Measuring your portfolio performance is not straight-forward. Investors tend to overstate their performance because of mathematical or psychological errors. Mathematical errors can include simple things like including the cash inflows as part of their returns. Psychological errors involve revising history: 'Oh, I had an off day when I picked those two stocks, I'll leave those out of my calcu-lations.'

How about some maths?

The maths is a little tricky. Imagine your $1,000 investment grows to $1,500 after three months (i.e. R1 = a 50 per cent gain). You then add another $1,000. The $2,500 then appreciates to $4,000 over the next nine months (R2 = 60 per cent gain). What is your total return?

Total return = R1 + R2 + R1xR2 or 0.5+0.6 + 0.5x0.6 = 140%

The total return is not simply the profit/capital, i.e. 2000/2000 (100 per cent) because your profit was earned on different amounts of capital. For instance, if you produced a 100 per cent return on $1,000 and then introduced $10,000 into your account on the last day of the year, your return is still virtually 100 per cent.

Having calculated my performance, how do I beat the fund managers?

Exploit the advantages of being small, explains Peter Siris in *Guerilla Investing* (1998, Longstreet Press). That often means small cap investments. See specialist site **www.itruffle.com** or **www.smallcapcenter.com** for small cap picks and news.

With billions to invest, many funds can't invest even 0.5 per cent of their capital without owning the company outright. If a fund's minimum investment is $300 million and the fund does not want to own more than 50 per cent of a company, then there's only 200 large cap public companies to choose from.

— www.stockhouse.com

Which stocks produce higher returns? Large or small companies?

Small cap stocks produce higher returns than large ones over a long time frame, according to research by Nobel prize winners Merton Miller and Myron Scholes. Moreover, Ben Warwick in *In Search of Alpha* (2000, John Wiley & Sons) confirms that with more money under management, pension funds confined to large caps find it increasingly difficult to generate alpha: market-beating returns.

As well as investing in small caps, how else can I beat the fund managers?

By adjusting the number of stocks in your portfolio. Robert Hagstrom's *The Warren Buffett Portfolio* (2000, John Wiley & Sons) explains that a portfolio with 250 stocks is less likely to beat the market than one with 15 stocks. But the fewer the stocks, the more volatile the returns (the beta) – i.e. the greater chance you will trail the market too.

> Buffett goes for the latter approach: 'Put all your eggs in one basket and watch the basket like a hawk'

Hagstrom suggests Buffett goes for the latter approach: 'Put all your eggs in one basket and watch the basket like a hawk.'

What if I cannot deal with alphas and betas, etc.?

If alpha and beta is all Greek to you, then of course consider investing through a fund manager, as should those who simply do not have the time or inclination to do their own stock picking. But don't be surprised if your civil engineer neighbour comes home from work in a Ferrari.

Where does past performance fit into stock picking?

All things being equal, should an online trader buy a stock that has doubled over the past year, or halved in value over that time frame?

I was asked this at a lecture, and it became clear that the answer is not as obvious to some as it is to me. Of course, all things are seldom equal, but it is a common dilemma among traders whether to focus on the shooting star stocks that just keep going up, or the dogs that just keep on drowning. It annoys me how many get the answer wrong. Equally interesting is what it reveals about them as traders and people.

The dilemma often starts like this: our first trader, let us call him Richard Traderman, is always on the look-out for stocks which are at their lows. His reasoning for buying into such stocks often falls into three fallacies.

The three fallacies if you will?

- The first fallacy is the 'if you burn it, they will come' fallacy. It goes like this: 'The stock cannot keep falling for ever, the sellers are likely to sell too much and their overreaction will see buyers flood in and the price rise.'

- The second fallacy is the 'white knight' fallacy, and the reasoning is thus: 'If the stock price does keep falling and the company gets cheaper, then someone is bound to come in and take the company over or institutional investors and shareholders will force a management restructure which will see the company share price rocket.'

- The final fallacy is the 'human infallibility' fallacy, which runs like this: 'I have an insight into the management and prospects of this company that the rest of the market has yet to see. Soon, clouds of ignorance will be removed from before the eyes of market makers and traders, and they too will see the light and the promised value this company surely deserves – according to me.'

So what would a smart trader do?

Our second trader, Alec Smart, always examines the share price trend first before even considering a stock purchase. He wants to see it rise smoothly upwards, with the stock becoming progressively more expensive in absolute terms each month.

Both Richard Traderman and Alec Smart want the same thing from their trading – they want to make money.

Who is more likely to be successful and why?

You may have guessed whose side I am on. In my view, it will almost always be Alec who will be the more successful.

First, while occasionally management overhauls occur and white knights appear, the timing is unpredictable. A stock can languish at depressingly low values for months, if not years, and companies do go bust. A tax write-off is not a legitimate investment strategy.

Second, you would sensibly want to diversify your holdings so that you are looking at maybe 10, possibly even 15 stocks to invest in. Any more than 15 stocks to monitor and it is unlikely you would have the time to keep an eye on them.

> The 'human infallibility' fallacy, which runs like this: 'I have an insight into the management and prospects of this company that the rest of the market has yet to see.'

What else can I learn from Traderman's poor strategy?

Another reason Traderman's strategy will fail him is that he is ignoring the singularly most important piece of information the market has about a stock: its price. And remember, the market is never wrong. To Richard Traderman, if the stock was worth buying at 100c, then if it halves to 50c, it is all the more cheaper, indeed attractive. If it should halve again he will buy some more at 25c – after all, now his average cost of purchase, and therefore his break-even point, is even lower.

What Traderman does not realize is that if the price is falling, stock holders are having to sell the stock at lower prices to find buyers. People just are not willing to pay any more. That should tell you something about what others think about the company. On the other hand, if the price of a stock is rising consistently, it indicates people are willing to pay more for it. There is likely to be market confidence in the company, and it is a good place to start further research into the stock, its earnings, newsflow, cashflow, market and sector.

What do I do when the stock plummets?

A good 'trailing stop' should limit that. So, for instance, you may have a rule that if the stock falls 20 per cent from its current level you will exit. There will be more about such risk and money management strategies later.

Richard Traderman is not real, but you will find his spirit in online chat rooms throughout the web. The poor souls are in share purgatory. To me it seems as if they may even get some perverse joy about worrying over their stock performance. Maybe they are punishing themselves? Or maybe they are congenital optimists. To these poor helpless souls I can give the advice of businessman Elbert Hubbard: 'The safest way to double your money is to fold it over once and put it in your pocket.'

Picking brokers

chapter eight

Online brokers not for all

Is online broking for everyone?

Too many investors are blindly opening online execution-only brokerage accounts when they would be better off with different forms of brokerage. Online execution-only brokers are ill-suited for many different types of investors. So while online brokers may seem as if they are trying to convince everyone that online trading is for them, you better read this chapter to see if you're one of the many for whom it is not suited.

> For those with little investment experience, execution-only brokers offer little support for making sound trading decisions

What if I am a market novice with some money set aside for investing?

For those with little investment experience, execution-only brokers offer little support for making sound trading decisions. No amount of market news, stock quotes, online portfolios and journalistic comment can replace the advice of a good, experienced broker for those unsure about investing.

What about an advisory broker?

> Although the advisory broker is nearly ten times more expensive, the market losses due to investor inexperience can be far greater

Advisory brokers require minimum account sizes of typically at least $10,000 and their commissions tend to be substantially greater than those of execution-only brokers because they are offering a personal added-value advisory service.

The commission costs of using a typical advisory broker such as Killik (**www.killik.com**), Pathburner (**www.pathburner.com**), or Durlacher (**www.durlacher.com**) on five $10,000 trades could be $825, compared with $87.50 in total with an execution-only broker such as Sharepeople (**www.sharepeople.com**).

However, consider the cost of losing 40 per cent of a $50,000 portfolio a market sell-off, compared with losing perhaps only 20 per cent because you used an experienced advisory broker. The saving in market losses would be $10,000. Therefore, although the advisory broker is nearly ten times more expensive, the market losses due to investor inexperience can be far greater. The cheaper DIY service of the deep-discount e-broker can be a false economy in a volatile or bearish market and an advisory broker can be a sound investment in itself for this type of investor.

What if I am relatively experienced and cash-rich?

Even the more experienced cash-rich investor may wish to have a second opinion from an advisory broker before committing a large sum of money to a stock decision based solely on his own research. Would it not make sense to pay an extra couple of hundred pounds for professional financial advice before committing, say, $50,000 of investment funds?

> Relatively lower-risk pooled financial products such as investment and unit trusts would allow them to tap into professional management at low cost

What to do for the cash-poor novice then?

Those who aren't confident about making their own trading decisions, and for whom the steep minimum account sizes and commission charges of advisory brokers don't make economic sense, should be considering longer-term investments, not short-term trading which requires them to rely frequently on their limited market knowledge.

Alternatively, relatively lower-risk pooled financial products such as investment and unit trusts would allow them to tap into professional management at low cost. 1-800-MUTUALS (**www.mutualfundworld.com**) bills itself as 'America's mutual fund superstore' and offers more than 7,000 funds as well as managed accounts; Brill's Mutual Funds Interactive (**www.brill.com**) offers news for all levels of investor and especially beginners; Morning Star (**www.morningstar.com**) offers top-notch research; Funds Direct (**www.fundsdirect.co.uk**), TrustNet (**www.trustnet.co.uk**), and MoneyExtra (**www.moneyextra.co.uk**) are good places to start.

But I am a sophisticated, highly active trader!

For those who are semi-professional in their trading, spending several hours each day monitoring the markets and looking to make several quick short trades daily, the services of an execution-only broker are likely to be inadequate. Such traders will require more than the low commission costs that e-brokers provide. They need lightning-fast execution that takes seconds, not minutes, and streaming real-time quotes. They need to consider dedicated trading platform software free from brokers such as Deal4Free (**www.deal4free.com**) and MyBroker (**www.mybroker.co.uk**) rather than purely a web-based service which executes orders through a glorified e-mail service, as seems to be the case with the tardy executions of e-brokers.

Such highly sophisticated traders who view stocks as just another short-term trading vehicle for profits will also want the choice of financial products that most e-brokers do not provide – forex trading, options and futures trading online. Again MyBroker and Deal4Free would be appropriate.

So for what type of investor is an online execution-only broker most suitable?

Ideally you would have market experience, be comfortable with making your own investment decisions, and be relatively active, making, say, at least two trades a month. You would be looking to hold your positions for at least several weeks and tend to have trade sizes of less than $7,000. Little wonder that market leaders Schwab and E*Trade are offering advisory services in the US because they can charge more for advice than execution only.

Figure 8.1 S&P composite, 1966–80

This 14-year bear market includes the crash of 1973–74

Adjusted for inflation, the S&P 500 did not return to its 1966 peak until 1991

Figure 8.2 S&P composite, 1906–24

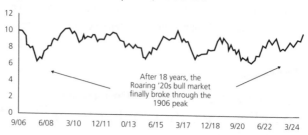

After 18 years, the
Roaring '20s bull market
finally broke through the
1906 peak

Just what type of broker is right for me?

So, since it feels as though there are almost as many online brokers as online traders, how does a wily online trader decide which broker to open an account with?

The factors to consider often enter the equation only after bitter experience. These are my conclusions. Of course, price is of primary concern. Online trading is popular partly because it offers discount commissions for investors who do not want to pay a full-fee broker for advice they could have discovered themselves on the internet, or for trades where they do not want advice.

But even among online brokers the commissions must vary? So which do I choose?

Well, commissions do vary greatly, but comparison is near impossible with each calculating commissions on a different basis – some using the value of your trade, others the number of shares bought, and others the frequency with which you trade. The best advice is to calculate what size trades you expect to make normally and then visit the various websites to work out who would offer you the cheapest commission.

Is there more to online trading than price?

Yes, there is certainly more to online broker selection than price – if there wasn't then Schwab in the US, which is one of the most expensive online brokers, would not have the largest market share. According to a study by JD Power and Associates, the most important factor in selecting an online broker is customer service. The same study, based on US brokers and traders only, found that Schwab topped the list for offering greatest customer satisfaction.

> There is certainly more to online broker selection than price.

Reliability?

Reliability in service is an essential prerequisite for any online trader. There is no point saving $20 in commission on buying a stock, only to find you can't sell it because your online broker has broken down. Such 'downtime' by online brokers is becoming increasingly frequent in the US, and in 2000 even the mighty Schwab had one full hour where trades could not be placed. In a survey by TheStreet.com (again a survey of US brokers by US clients), DLJ Direct came top in the category of reliability. They are now owned by TDWaterhouse.com

So execution is important then?

Poor execution can also override price as a concern for an online trader. The price at which your trade is 'executed' should be as close as possible to the real-time price quote you see on the screen before you trade. Poor execution can often end up swamping any commission savings. In the TheStreet.com survey, Schwab came above DLJ Direct, which in turn narrowly beat E*Trade on the issue of execution prices.

If you like such almost-scientific surveys of online brokers, see **www.gomez.com**. The website's internet broker 'overall score' rankings placed E*Trade in pole position, with DLJ Direct and Schwab in second and third place respectively.

What about the look of the site?

Site design is an important consideration for me. There is nothing worse when you are trying to find a quote, do some research or quickly place a trade than to find navigation around the site as difficult as travelling up the Amazon (the river, not the site). I want my online broker easy and intuitive to use. There is only one way to see what suits you and that is to visit the sites themselves. I am sorry to report that I find the purely UK online brokers, unlike US brokers with UK sites, seem too often to be competing for the title of most offputting site, and that's when they are not racing to see who can be the most expensive. Did these site designers speak to a single online trader?

> Online trading is about more than placing a trade through an online broker instead of phoning a traditional broker. Trading online profitably still requires research to arrive at stock picks, and the internet is an excellent resource to offer this

Online trading is about more than placing a trade through an online broker instead of phoning a traditional broker. Trading online profitably still requires research to arrive at stock picks, and the internet is an excellent resource to offer this. I always check to see what research the online brokers offer.

Do they provide free portfolio monitoring, charting, news from major wires, research from renowned institutions and commentary, or are they just a website appended to a traditional brokerage?

All in all I much prefer the big US brokers' UK sites to the sites of purely UK brokers because of site design, commission and available research. When it comes to choosing between the US brokers themselves, I prefer the biggest players like the ones mentioned above (and for that matter below) because it is they, with their leverage and clout, who can offer quality research and the security of knowing they have the money to spend on resources.

Sites?

Try the following: **www.etrade.com** (in addition to the broker service, it offers a load of free tools to the public such as real-time quotes, customizable portfolios, personalized market views and e-mail), **www.eschwab.com**, **www.datek.com** and **www.scottrade.com**.

For Latin American trading check out Patagon at **www.patagon.com** and Latin Stocks at **www.latinstocks.com.ar** (Argentina), **www.latinstocks.com.br** (Brazil) and **www.latinstocks.com.mx** (Mexico).

Note how analysts can get it wrong, recommending buying a stock as it keeps falling (Fig 9.1)

Figure 9.1 Morgan Stanley's early call helped it nab the best Amazon return

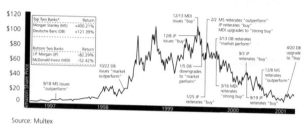

Source: Multex

It seems analysts have a bias towards saying 'buy'. So be warned if you follow them and not your own research (Fig 9.2).

Figure 9.2 Distribution of outstanding analyst recommendations

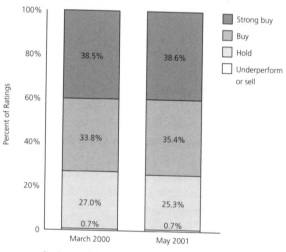

Based on an analysis of total outstanding analyst recommendations on
March 24 2000 and May 4 2001
Source: Industry Standard June 2001

Fig 9.3 shows how, even as the market falls, analysts continue giving the buy recommendation.

Figure 9.3 New tech stock analyst ratings vs Nasdaq performance

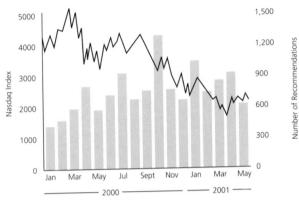

Source: Industry Standard

Even the 19 largest brokerages have issued money-losing stock advice, according to investment research firm Investars.com. Even the bank with the best overall credit rating – Credit Suisse First Boston – had returns below 7 percent for traders following its advice precisely. Another reason to pick your own stocks?

Figure 9.4 Hypothetical investment return based on analyst recommendations

All Stocks

Top 5	Investment Bank or Research Firm	Stocks Rated	Return
1	Credit Suisse First Boston	1,558	+6.9%
2	A.G. Edwards	600	+4.4%
3	Salomon Smith Barney	1,348	+0.9%
4	Merrill Lynch	1,491	–1.5%
5	Morgan Stanley	1,184	–2.7%

Bottom 5			
1	Robertson Stephens	693	–48.3%
2	USB Piper Jaffray	617	–22.7%
3	Dain Rauscher	627	–21.5%
4	CBC World Markets	804	–14.7%
5	Deutsche Banc	804	–14.7%

Technology Hardware Stocks

Top 5	Investment Bank or Research Firm	Stocks Rated	Return
1	Merrill Lynch	143	–13.59%
2	Bear Stearns	100	–18.3%
3	A.G. Edwards	55	–18.7%
4	Salomon Smith Barney	149	–18.8%
5	Goldman Sachs	11	–18.3%

Bottom 5			
1	Robertson Stephens	153	–54.9%
2	Dain Rauscher	96	–54.4%
3	Deutsche Banc	90	–51.4%
4	USB Piper Jaffray	82	–50.9%
5	USB PaineWebber	85	–47.1%

Source: Industry Standard

chapter ten

Why do so many traders have the wrong broker?

Can online discount brokers offer advice?

Remember too that online discount brokers cannot offer advice because by law they are restricted to being execution only. While they may offer news feeds, which can include broker recommendations, for truly detailed analysis and the highest quality investment ideas nothing can beat the analysis of 'the best on the street', as long as you can get it for free.

For truly detailed analysis and the highest quality investment ideas nothing can beat the analysis of 'the best on the street', as long as you can get it for free

What are full-service brokers offering now that online discount brokers are offering free research?

In response to the growth in discount online brokers, Merrill Lynch has been the highest-profile traditional full-fee broker to offer online trading and open its gates to its highly prized research, which is still available for free from **http://askmerrill.com/international**.

Name some more names then.

Another full-service broker forced by the competition from online brokers to offer its research to the public is Paine Webber, which has an excellent service at **www.painewebber.com**, offering equity, market, industry and thematic research.

Then there's the mighty Salomon Smith Barney at **www.salomonsmithbarney.com** offering worldwide research from a macroeconomic to individual equity level, plus my favourite, special reports on internet and technology stocks generally. And none of this is second-rate findings from a trainee that the company deigns worthy of giving away for free just before binning it – it is good quality stuff I would gladly scour the bins outside their offices for.

Lehman Brothers also cuts to the chase and lists its ten 'uncommon value' stock picks at **www.lehman.com**.

Who's really good?

When it comes to top-quality internet and technology stocks research available free on the web, no one beats Morgan Stanley Dean Witter in my opinion. You can find excellent and hefty reports at **www.ms.com**. The downside is that the download will take for ever and a good few trees as there are hundreds of pages in each report. Try saving them to hard disk and save the forests. You should also try Merrill Lynch HSBC (**MLHSBC.com**) who provide free reports to clients.

What if I want the top full-service brokers – how much will it cost me?

Of course there are many people who do not want to do their own research or to trade through a discount online broker and prefer relying on a full-service broker for advice, not just free research; so much so that Merrill's web account attracts about $3 billion in new assets each quarter, while the execution-only broker Charles Schwab (**www.eschwab.com**) attracts $30 billion per quarter according to industry sources.

If you are tempted to use a top full-service broker such as Merrill Lynch, you will find fees as a retail customer of more than $50 per trade, and sometimes as high as $200 – far higher than the $5 to $30 charged by discount online brokers. Merrill combines broker advice and online trading in an account charging $1,500 minimum p.a. For that you get not only research but advice.

What are clever online traders doing?

Keep a regular watch on the sites of the full-service brokers mentioned above. Use the free research they provide to place trades 'on the cheap' through execution-only brokers

Given that John Steffens, head of Merrill's retail business, estimates that the average customer has between $350,000 and $450,000 in their new full-service web trading accounts, whereas a survey by TheStreet.Com reveals that most online discount broker account holders trade with less than $5,000, it may be that wily traders make the big decisions with the advice of the big brokers and rely on their own judgements with small amounts.

So what's your advice then?

Keep a regular watch on the sites of the full-service brokers mentioned above. Use the free research they provide to place trades 'on the cheap' through execution-only brokers.

Portfolio and risk management

chapter eleven

What do I need to know about my portfolio that the professionals know?

How do I find out how likely it is that my portfolio will drop a stomach-churning amount?

A stock portfolio is possibly your second largest investment, after your home. Even a single stock investment of $6,000 is perhaps the largest single purchase a net trader makes all year. But we don't know our portfolios, beyond the names of the stocks within them, their share prices and maybe a few news stories about the companies.

> A stock portfolio is possibly your second largest investment, after your home.

Some net traders use online portfolio trackers, such as that on **www.etrade.com** or **www.datek.com**, to track their profits and losses, receiving daily e-mail updates of their holdings and all news relating to their holdings that

now www.tdameritrade.com

day. Frankly, we don't know the likelihood of our portfolio dropping a stomach-churning amount. We need to know. This chapter tells us how.

Should I use software to monitor my portfolio?

Traditionalists will use portfolio monitoring software such as Quicken (**www.quicken.com**), Microsoft Money or a spreadsheet program such as Excel to keep tabs on their holdings, or go to a portal such as the excellent Yahoo!Finance (**www.yahoo.com**). But this is basic.

So what is better?

Newer online tools mean we should have far greater technical knowledge on a par with professional money managers about how our portfolios behave.

What should I know?

How much money could you lose because of extreme market movements, say where price fluctuations exceed 95 per cent of the typical daily price changes? Before the internet such calculations would have been outside the competency of most net traders. After all, you would need to look at the daily performance of the stock on each business day of the previous year (on average, 252 business days), then rank the daily returns from lowest to highest. Next you would need to calculate the average of the worst 5 per cent of the daily returns (or, approximately, the worst 13 of the 252 return values).

Why is this important?

It could mean the difference between a portfolio whose risk appetite you can stomach and one that leaves you taking risks far greater than you anticipated. If you can anticipate the types of losses your individual holdings and overall portfolio may typically incur, you can decide whether to reduce or rebalance your holdings.

> It could mean the difference between a portfolio whose risk appetite you can stomach and one that leaves you taking risks far greater than you anticipated

So how healthy is your portfolio?

Apologies from CEOs for poor shareholder returns is commonplace, but not when the CEO is Warren Buffett. The closure of hedge funds is common, but not the flagship funds of George Soros. Trading losses too are no surprise, but not from the personal portfolio of the head of a trading firm (Track Data) and amounting to $45 million!

So what chance do I, a private investor, stand of making good returns in turbulent markets if even the most experienced are suffering poor investment performance?

Is my portfolio underperforming relative to key benchmarks such as the S&P 500 or the FTSE 100 and indeed which benchmarks should I be targeting?

Other questions that crop up along the same lines include, Do I have the optimal mix of stocks, cash and other financial assets for my risk profile and financial goals? and How do I know if I own too few or too many stocks for the risk/reward I am targeting?

It's not surprising that such questions arise given that existing financial portals have hardly developed innovative portfolio tools in the past several years despite an increase in competition between sites.

Sure, simple online portfolio tracking, which updates stock prices but little else, offered by sites such as E*Trade (**www.etrade.com**) or Stocktrade (**www.stocktrade.co.uk**) is useful in allowing online traders to more quickly and easily monitor their holdings, but as with the display of quantitative financial information, online portfolio tools reveal a lack of understanding of customer needs and of creativity. We don't even have pie charts to show the relative weightings of our holdings or bar charts to depict their relative performances.

For an answer to these questions, two of the best sites and tools can be found at **www.quicken.com** and **www.riskgrades.com**.

What do I need?

Asset allocation tools are one major category of online portfolio tools that are important but often lacking, yet they are relatively easy and inexpensive to provide. Asset allocation analysis involves determining the financial goals, time horizon, risk tolerance, tax status and investing experience of an individual and suggesting asset classes that the investor should hold, e.g. large, mid and small cap stock holdings, cash, fixed income and international securities .

What else?

Tax analysis providing running income and capital gains tax liability reports (and allowing for indexation allowances) is another service that is easy to provide but often missing on financial portals.

How do I know how well my portfolio is doing?

Another aspect of portfolio analysis missing from online portfolios is performance analysis. While online portfolios of brokers like Ameritrade (**www.ameritrade.com**) and Stocktrade (**www.stocktrade.com**) and portals such as ADVFN (**www.advfn.com**) provide some useful portfolio performance information such as total gross profit or loss and individual percentage gains since purchase, they lack further analytical tools. For those I suggest **www.quicken.com**.

In analyzing performance what should I look for?

The following would be useful:

■ the ratio of winning to losing trades;

■ the average holding periods for each, so for instance one could determine whether losing stocks are being held for too short a time and losses could therefore be minimized by exiting trades later;

■ annualized returns based on current performance;

■ commission paid, including the average amount per trade (there may be an opportunity to maintain return but reduce commissions by altering the size or number of trades);

■ the maximum favourable and adverse excursion, i.e. the highest and lowest value the overall portfolio reaches as well as individual stocks so that one can gauge the reward-to-risk prospects of the portfolio and stocks;

■ a measure of the correlation between individual stocks to help gauge the extent of diversification.

Even without online portfolio tools offering the above, the serious investor should monitor the above information manually or on a spread-sheet.

But this is too difficult, isn't there anything else I can do?

What the lack of detailed valuable analytical tools combined with recent market losses reveals is that some individuals would be far better with advisory brokers rather than execution-only ones. Realizing this, discount brokers in the US, led by E*Trade and Schwab, are offering advisory services which also allow the online brokers to break out of the low margin and high marketing cost execution-only segment of the market and enter the more lucrative higher margin advisory brokerage market.

> **Even without online portfolio tools offering the above the serious investor should monitor information manually or on a spread-sheet**

Although it is unlikely that their offering of advisory services is motivated by customer care, and is in fact rather a concern for the 'bottom line', if e-brokers offered some of those portfolio tools as part of their execution-only services they would improve customer investment performance and ultimately keep more of them – thereby improving their own and their customers' profitability. Of course, lessons from Buffett and Soros suggest any improvements are not guaranteed to be easy or indefinite.

What is risk?
How do I quickly and easily measure it like a professional trader?

I don't want to maximize my returns from trading online. If at the start of the tech boom in 1999 I had invested, say, $10,000 equally between the five best performing TMTs, I would probably have well over $30,000. But I am not losing sleep over having missed them.

> I want to maximize my reward-to-risk ratio

Why?

I want to maximize my reward-to-risk ratio and buying those stocks would not have done that.

How can I measure the risk I am exposed to?

Even those who have some idea about risk use outdated, unsophisticated or discredited measures. Beta is a popular yet incomplete measure of risk. Beta measures how much an individual stock is likely to move with the general market. A beta of 1 means that a stock will tend to move lock step with the general market, while a beta of 2 means that the stock will rise 2 per cent for any 1 per cent rise in the stock market, and fall 2 per cent with any 1 per cent fall in the stock market, on average.

What's wrong with beta?

Beta can be misleading. For instance, two stocks with the same beta generally have a different level of risk. Standard deviation is another common measure of risk and it too has deficiencies. For example, it fails to weight historical share prices to give more significance to the most recent prices.

What other risk management tools are there then?

Newer online tools remove traditional problems with risk measurement because the internet tools do the complicated calculations for you real-time. This will potentially result in greater online trading returns. JP Morgan has taken its internationally and institutionally acclaimed RiskMetrics risk calculations and converted them for the private investor through RiskGrades (**www.riskgrades.com**).

This is a very powerful tool. It reveals, for instance, that two stocks can be equally risky (in very simple terms they have been equally volatile in the past six months), yet the one-year returns can be very different.

What else can RiskGrades do?

RiskGrades also suggests online traders have riskier stock portfolios than they realize. Consequently their returns are often lower than they expect – losses greater than anticipated or profits lower than they should be. The problem is so great that even model portfolios on reputable websites misjudge the level of risk they advocate.

> Inconsistencies can exist in many portfolios, even brokers' model portfolios

Inconsistencies can exist in many portfolios, even brokers' model portfolios. The fault is not theirs. It is due to a general lack of understanding of the nature of risk and an unnecessarily intuitive not quantitative approach to risk.

If inconsistencies in how I handle risk can arise in my portfolio, what should I do to correct them?

I suggest the serious private investor should know the following about their stock portfolios:

- which stocks contribute the greatest risk to their portfolio;
- how well diversified their portfolio is;

- what you should expect to see as an average worst case one-day trading loss;
- whether replacing any stocks reduces risk without impacting return, or even improving it.
- how to use RiskGrades to evaluate the above for your portfolio.

Since risk and diversification go hand in hand, how many stocks should a well-diversified portfolio contain?

As few as a dozen stocks can yield good diversification. A diversified portfolio is one where the negative impact on a portfolio of an event due solely to a specific stock is minimized.

What about the type of stocks I choose?

All important in diversification are the stocks you select

All important in diversification are the stocks you select. Again, too many private investors have stocks closely correlated to each other. Simply buying a stock from different sectors is not the answer because sectors can be linked in their movements too. RiskGrades allows quick assessment of how diversified your portfolio is.

So, if I'm not maximizing my returns per se, what am I maximizing?

The trick with a portfolio is to maximize reward for any level of risk through asset allocation. According to RiskGrades an aggressive portfolio can produce an expected annual return of 30 per cent, but that is only if the assets are allocated to minimize risk.

I would rather underperform and have a better risk-to-reward ratio than be a star performer taking great risks. Trading is not a one-shot game and in the long term I would be the outperformer.

> I would rather underperform and have a better risk-to-reward ratio than be a star performer taking great risks. Trading is not a one-shot game and in the long term I would be the outperformer

But what if I am tempted by those risky tech stocks?

Unfortunately many traders first select risky 'growth' internet stocks, reasoning that if they are risky then growth will follow. Such fallacious reasoning is equivalent to saying 'if producing high-grade steel results in pollution, therefore if I pollute I will produce high-grade steel'. Consequently they have all the risk but little of the return because of the assets selected. Once again the online tools of RiskGrade assist in resolving that problem.

The bottom line?

Too few private investor websites understand online trading. If they did they would provide as many statistics about risk as they do about P/E ratios. Doubtless brokers will provide such information with the motive of encouraging greater trades as investors rejig their portfolios in pursuit of the ideal portfolio. E-traders need to be aware that the risk of overtrading and incurring commission costs from doing so that is not measured by RiskGrades.

> **E-traders need to beware the risk of overtrading**

How much risk can I take?

Know thyself. It is essential that as an investor you know how much risk you can tolerate. If you are quite conservative, you may be averse to the probability that the market may fall 5 per cent. An aggressive investor, however, may take a 5 per cent drop with a pinch of salt since he thinks there is a good probability of a 5 or 10 per cent rise. The exercise below will help you know yourself.

EXERCISE – RISK TOLERANCE TEST

An investor's risk tolerance in making investment decisions can depend on investment goals as well as the investor's personality. The following exercise will measure your reaction to market risk, weight the relative importance of your goals and uncover your personal investment preferences.

109

WHAT IS RISK? HOW DO I QUICKLY AND EASILY MEASURE IT LIKE A PROFESSIONAL TRADER?

Give yourself the points in the brackets for your answer.

1. The degree to which the value of an investment moves up and down is referred to as 'volatility'. In general, more volatile investments tend to grow faster than more stable investments – they have a larger potential upside. However, volatile investments are more risky since there is no guarantee that the 'upturns' will be larger than the 'downturns'. How much volatility are you willing to accept?

   A Slight. I do not want to lose money, even if it means my returns are small. (1)

   B Some. I am willing to accept the occasional loss as long as my money is in sound, high-quality investments that can be expected to grow over time. (3)

   C Considerable. I am willing to take substantial risk in pursuit of significantly higher returns. (5)

TOTAL POINTS _____

2. Suppose your investment portfolio contains a significant portion of large company stocks in addition to several other assets. Large company stocks have averaged a compound annual return of 11 per cent over the past 72 years. However, if large company stocks had lost 18 per cent of their value in the past year, what would you do?

A Sell the large company stock portion of my investment portfolio and realize the loss. (1)

B Sell some, but not all, of the large company stock portion. (2)

C Continue to hold the large company stock portion of my investment portfolio, following a consistent long-term strategy. (3)

D Buy more large company stocks. (4)

TOTAL POINTS _____

3. Please provide your response to the following statement.

   Given my investment time horizon, I am willing to accept significant fluctuations in the value of my investments to achieve potentially higher long-term returns.

   A Strongly disagree. (0)

   B Disagree. (1)

   C Agree. (2)

   D Strongly agree. (5)

TOTAL POINTS _____

4. Which of the following statements is most true about your risk tolerance and the way you wish to invest to achieve your goal(s)? My investment should...

111

WHAT IS RISK? HOW DO I QUICKLY AND EASILY MEASURE IT LIKE A PROFESSIONAL TRADER?

A be completely safe; I do not wish to run the risk of losing any principal at any time. (1)

B generate regular income that I can spend. (2)

C generate some current income and also grow in value over time. (3)

D grow over time, but I would also like to generate some current income. (4)

E grow substantially in value over time. I do not need to generate current income. (5)

TOTAL POINTS _____

5. An investor must be prepared to expose his/her investments to increased chances of loss in attempting to achieve higher expected returns. The following statements represent possible outcomes for three hypothetical portfolios at the end of one year. Which investment portfolio would you be most comfortable holding?

A Portfolio A has a likely return of 6 per cent, and there is a 10 per cent chance of loss at the end of the year. (2)

B Portfolio B has a likely return of 10 per cent, and there is an 18 per cent chance of loss at the end of the year. (3)

C Portfolio C has a likely return of 14 per cent, and there is a 25 per cent chance of loss at the end of the year. (4)

TOTAL POINTS _____

6. I understand the value of my portfolio will fluctuate over time. However, the maximum loss in any one-year period that I am prepared to accept is:

A 0 per cent. (1)
B −5 per cent. (2)
C −10 per cent. (3)
D −20 per cent.
E −30 per cent+. (5)

TOTAL POINTS _____

7. Investments in which the principal is '100 per cent safe' sometimes earn less than the inflation rate. This means that, while no money is lost, there is a loss of purchasing power. With respect to your goal(s), which of the following is most true?

A My money should be '100 per cent safe' even if it means my returns do not keep up with inflation. (0)

B It is important that the value of my investments keeps pace with inflation. I am willing to risk an occasional loss in principal so that my investments may grow at about the same rate as inflation over time. (3)

C It is important that my investments grow faster than inflation. I am willing to accept a fair amount of risk to try to achieve this. (5)

TOTAL POINTS _____

8. Which statement best describes your main concern when selecting an investment?

A The potential for loss.   (1)

B Mostly the potential for loss, but also the potential for gain. (2)

C Mostly the potential for gain, but I am still concerned about the potential for loss. (3)

D The potential for gain.   (4)

TOTAL POINTS_____

9. Consider the following two investments, A and B. Investment A provides an average annual return of 7 per cent with minimal risk of loss of principal. Investment B provides an average annual return of 10 per cent but carries a potential loss of principal of 20 per cent or more in any one year. If I could choose between Investment A and Investment B to meet my goal(s), I would invest my money:

A 100 per cent in A and 0 per cent in B. (1)

B 75 per cent in A and 25 per cent in B. (2)

C 50 per cent in A and 50 per cent in B. (3)

D 25 per cent in A and 75 per cent in B. (4)

E 0 per cent in A and 100 per cent in B. (5)

TOTAL POINTS _____

If you tended to go for the first options in the above questions, you are quite averse to risk. So, if you scored between

- 8 and 20 you tend to be particularly risk-averse;

- 21 and 35 you tend to be neutral towards risk and volatility;

- 36 and 50 you like market volatility, regarding it as the best opportunity to make money.

Does investing online lessen the risk of losing money?

Investing online can lessen risk but only to the extent that it puts all the tools and resources in your hands to conveniently make your own investing decisions. When you're online, you can easily scan the market indicators and price-track movements, thus reducing the risk of error of judgement.

Interest rate risk

When the cost of borrowing money goes up, it erodes the value of certain investments since it reduces the relative return on the investments. This is especially vigorous for long-term fixed securities like bonds. For example, if you bought a bond with the 'fantastic' rate of 8 per cent and five years later interest rates move above 8 per cent, you will have a lower relative return compared to, say, savings accounts.

Investor psychology

Panicky investors' overreaction to fluctuating interest rates and inflation fears prompts a market sell-off that affects the value of investments, even among those who kept their heads. Herding behaviour can create exceptionally volatile markets.

Market conditions

Stock prices can soar to such highs per dollar invested that the market and your individual investments become more vulnerable in the event of a decline. This is also referred to as market indices.

Liquidity

A liquidity risk is the inability to convert an investment quickly and easily to cash, which is purely liquid, without incurring a significant loss in the value of the investment.

Any tips for trading in Latin America?

■ ZonaFinanciera (**www.zonafinanciera.com**) gives you a good picture of the economic climate in Latin America and an idea of general market risk. What makes this site particularly useful is that it is very broad in terms of the number of countries it covers. The site offers separate, detailed information for all the major Latin American markets: Argentina, Bolivia, Brazil, Chile, Colombia, Costa Rica, Ecuador, El Salvador, Spain, Guatemala, Honduras, Mexico, Nicaragua, Panama, Paraguay, Peru, Puerto Rico, the Dominican Republic, Uruguay and Venezuela.

Under the stocks section there is a complete review of the main developments in the markets and you can trade online in stocks and mutual funds. Market commentary is knowledgeable.

Alongside key indicators such as quick quotes, indices, currency and news reports, there is an interesting section, 'Investor School', that provides information on the basics as well as on strategic investing and risk assessment.

■ Bloomberg Latin America (**www.bloomberg.com/sa**) is quite general and offers only basic information about the major Latin American indices and financial news.

■ LatinInvestor (**www.latininvestor.com**) has a wide range of authoritative reports from brokers and consulting firms on the major Latin American economies, companies and industries. Key market information is available on Argentina, Brazil, Chile, Mexico, Peru and Venezuela. However, only a small number of these reports are free.

Figure 12.1 Some good news: here's a list of significant events and how they have affected the markets. As you can see, one year later the markets had returned to positive returns, except for 1981–82.

	Date	Event	First Trading Session Response to Event				Subsequent Market Behaviour		
			DJIA Close Previous Day	DJIA Close	DJIA Change	DJIA % Change	One Month Change	Six Month Change	One Year Change
1.	1/17/91	US launches bombing attack on Iraq	2,509	2,624	114.6	**4.6%**	11.8%	15.0%	**24.5%**
2.	8/2/90	Iraq invades Kuwait	2,899	2,865	–34.7	**–1.2%**	–8.8%	–3.2%	**5.0%**
3.	3/30/81	President Reagan shot	995	992	–2.6	**–0.3%**	0.6%	–14.3%	**–16.9%**
4.	8/9/74	President Nixon resigns	785	777	–7.6	**–0.97%**	–14.7%	–8.9%	**6.0%**
5.	11/22/63	President Kennedy assassinated	733	711	–21.2	**–2.9%**	6.6%	15.4%	**25.0%**
6.	10/22/62	Cuban Missile Crisis	569	558	–10.5	**–1.9%**	15.6%	27.4%	**34.0%**
7.	9/26/55	President Eisenhower heart attack	487	456	–31.9	**–6.5%**	0.04%	12.5%	**5.7%**
8.	6/25/50	North Korea invades South Korea	224	214	–10.4	**–4.7%**	–4.5%	7.4%	**15.1%**
9.	12/7/41	Japan attacks Pearl Harbor, Hawaii	117	113	–4.1	**–3.5%**	–0.9%	–6.2%	**2.9%**

Source: **dowjones.com**

Past performance is not a guarantee of future performance.

chapter thirteen

Why do I want to invest in bonds and what is the best way for me?

What is a bond?

A bond is a loan to a government, corporation or other entity known as the issuer. In return for the loan, the issuer promises to pay you a specified rate of interest during the life of the bond and to repay the face value of the bond (the principal) when it 'matures'.

Among the types of bonds you can choose from are government securities, municipal bonds, corporate bonds and foreign government bonds. The safe-haven, low-risk, guaranteed returns offered by government bonds are overlooked by too many online investors.

> The safe-haven, low-risk, guaranteed returns offered by government bonds are overlooked by too many online investors

An example, please?

Bonds should form an essential part of a balanced planned portfolio. You would alter the mix of cash, bonds and stock to fit the desired goal and risk tolerance

The $100 Treasury 6 per cent 2002 bond may trade in the market at $98. It will pay two interest payments during the year of $3 each (6 per cent of $100). The government guarantees this and a payment of $100 on maturity in 2002 – a $2 return above today's purchase price.

But you can also buy and sell gilts in the open market during the period between the issue and redemption date. If you do this, you may make a capital gain or loss.

Why should you consider the lowest risk bonds – government/Treasury bonds or gilts – as part of your online trading portfolio?

Guaranteed returns is a key attraction – sacrificing the possibly greater reward of holding equities for the certainty of a positive return and the guarantee of no loss. In a volatile climate would you prefer a guaranteed 10 per cent return from bonds or an uncertain return from a tech stock?

So, how should bonds fit into my overall investment portfolio?

Bonds should form an essential part of a balanced planned portfolio. You would alter the mix of cash, bonds and stock to fit the desired goal and risk tolerance.

How should I divide my portfolio in terms of bonds, shares and cash?

That will depend on your particular preferences to risk (see Chapter 12). A *Wall Street Journal* survey of portfolio strategists at 13 top brokerage firms showed they recommended a portfolio blend of assets that includes 31 per cent bonds, 61 per cent stocks and 6 per cent cash.

But what if I am quite conservative?

If you are rather risk-averse then you will go for a higher proportion of bond (and cash) vis-a-vis shares (Fig 13.1). A conservative plan, with income from stock dividends and portfolio value stability exchanged for potential upside, would probably involve 25 per cent in cash, 20 per cent in stocks and 55 per cent in bonds, according to Charles Schwab (**www.eschwab.com**).

Figure 13.1 A conservative plan

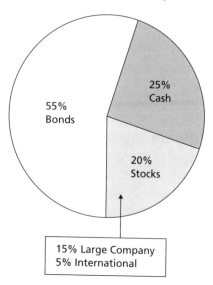

25%
Cash

55%
Bonds

20%
Stocks

15% Large Company
5% International

Return (1970–2000)
- Average annual return: 9.32%
- Best year: 21.81%
- Worst year: −1.25%

How would a conservative portfolio perform?

The conservative portfolio averaged 9.32 per cent annually between 1970 and 1999, with 22 per cent in its best year and a mere −1.25 per cent in the worst year. Your choice of portfolio is determined by your financial goals and risk tolerance. Figure 13.2 shows a moderately conservative plan.

Figure 13.2 A moderately conservative plan

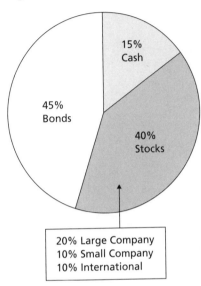

15%
Cash

45%
Bonds

40%
Stocks

20% Large Company
10% Small Company
10% International

Return (1970–2000)
- Average annual return: 10.52%
- Best year: 25.56%
- Worst year: –6.55%

What about an aggressive, risk-preferring portfolio?

An aggressive portfolio would hold 95 per cent in stocks, according to Schwab (probably 30 per cent in international stocks, 25 per cent small companies and 40 per cent large companies), and the remainder in cash (Fig 13.3).

Figure 13.3 An aggressive plan

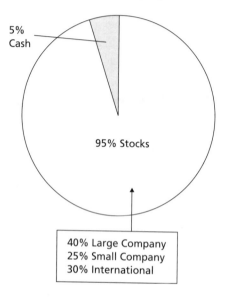

5%
Cash

95% Stocks

40% Large Company
25% Small Company
30% International

Return (1970–2000)
- Average annual return: 12.80%
- Best year: 42.25%
- Worst year: −23.83%

And how would it perform?

According to Schwab, between 1970 and 1999 such a plan would typically yield 12.80 per cent annually, the best year producing 42 per cent and the worst a loss of 24 per cent. This plan is for long-term investors who want high growth and don't need current income. Substantial year-to-year volatility in value is exchanged for potentially high long-term returns. Figure 13.4 shows a moderately aggressive plan.

125

WHY DO I WANT TO INVEST IN BONDS AND WHAT IS THE BEST WAY FOR ME?

Figure 13.4 A moderately aggressive plan

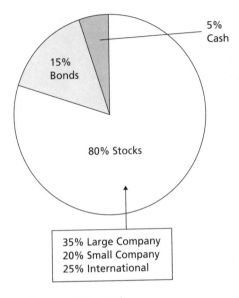

5%
Cash

15%
Bonds

80% Stocks

35% Large Company
20% Small Company
25% International

Return (1970–2000)
- Average annual return: 12.32%
- Best year: 36.52%
- Worst year: −19.14%

I still don't know what the mix of stock to bonds to cash should be. Any other methods of allocating a portfolio?

This one is not very scientifically rigorous, but here goes… one method for allocating a retirement portfolio suggests that you subtract your age from 100. The resulting number is how much of your portfolio should be invested in stocks.

For example, if you are 35 years old, 100 − 35 = 65, so 65 per cent of your portfolio could be allocated to stocks, 25 per cent to bonds and a constant 10 per cent to cash.

Are there any other benefits to bonds?

Aside from the risk/reward enhancement to a portfolio, another benefit of investing in bonds is the active secondary market for gilts which means they can be readily traded before maturity if you need cash unexpectedly. Such liquidity offers a flexibility you won't get from high-yielding bank accounts.

Are bonds complicated investment tools?

Financial and tax planning with bonds requires professional advice for most people. There is a lack of financial planning tools that actually ask your financial goals – the amount you want to raise, your risk tolerance, how much you have in savings – then suggest the optimal combination of bonds, stocks and cash based on past market performance. In the meantime, visit MoneyExtra's (**www.moneyextra.co.uk**) IFA search to find an Independent Financial Advisor near you.

However, there are loads of educational resources…

Websites?

To invest in US Treasuries visit **www.investinginbonds.com**. This provides very good practical and educational tools with in-depth explanations of different types of bonds, as well as a seven-step educational programme. **www.bondsonline.com** includes data on federal, municipal and corporate bonds. Many US brokers, such as **www.Ameritrade.com**, offer online bond trading, as do some US brokers in the UK such as **www.schwab-europe.com**. However, such brokers do not offer online trading of UK gilts.

Are there any other ways I could access the bond market?

Bond funds are another way to access the bond market. They offer the added diversification of a pooled investment. Visit Interactive Investor International (**www.iii.co.uk**) for past performance of funds. The site also covers the higher risk corporate bond market. Truly the name is bond, government bond.

> Bond funds are another way to access the bond market. They offer the added diversification of a pooled investment

Any more sites?

Of course. **www.taxfreebond.com** provides online bond brokerage and offers free research tools, including municipal bond primer and taxable equivalent yield calculators.

Others include:

■ **www.bondtrac.com** – offers handy free search tools.

■ **www.bradynet.com** – *the* site for getting info about

Brady bonds, the Third World debt instruments issued by the US government.

- **www.publicdebt.treas.gov** – the Bureau of the Public Debt.

- **www.moodys.com** is the Moody's Investor Services that pours forth masses of research on companies and publishes a lot of it on the web for free.

What about Latin America?

For Latin America, Patagon **www.patagon.com** offers bond trading and funds for all the major markets. Also, BradyNet **www.bradynet.com** provides specific information on Brady bonds for Mexico, Ecuador, Argentina, Venezuela and Brazil. There are market commentaries, a research library, and individual company profiles. Charting and technical analysis is informative, but available only once registered.

Active trading

chapter fourteen

Should I trade actively? Which are the best tools and what do the wrong ones cost me?

I am an active trader, trading around three times a day. Can use a normal online broker like, say, E*Trade or Schwab?

For a serious active internet trader the services of the most popular online brokers will not do. These browser-based brokers cannot compare to specialist brokers. Recent innovations are the by-product of the day-trading craze, yet should be considered a necessity to a far wider audience.

> If you need fast trade executions a browser-based broker will prove frustratingly inadequate

Why do I need a 'special broker'?

If you need fast trade executions in seconds not minutes, detailed price quotes – telling you who is in the queue to buy or sell your stock and at what prices – speedy order entry, real-time balance adjustments, institutional quality trading screens and analytical information, then a browser-based broker will prove frustratingly inadequate.

What is the difference then between a browser-based broker and an active broker?

Browser-based brokers such as the market leaders – Schwab (**www.eschwab.com** or **www.schwab-europe.com**), E*Trade (**www.etrade.com** or **www.etrade.co.uk**), TD Waterhouse (**www.tdwaterhouse.co.uk**), Datek (**www.datek.com**) and Pathburner (**www.pathburner.com**) – differ from active trader brokers in significant ways. Each of these makes browser-based brokerage inadequate for the active net trader. Essentially, browser-based brokers are slower and less streamlined than active brokers in providing such services as quote updates, execution and order entry.

Why are active brokers faster in providing quote updates?

When you seek an update intra-day price chart from a browser-based broker your request passes from your PC, via the internet, to the broker's server. The server finds the quote, rebuilds the web page on which to display the

133

SHOULD I TRADE ACTIVELY? WHICH ARE THE BEST TOOLS AND WHAT DO THE WRONG ONES COST ME?

chart, and passes it back to your PC via the net. Delays often occur with the server or on the internet due to the amount of traffic.

However, active trader brokers offer a faster service. They provide software that resides on your PC and does calculations, such as constructing charts and your portfolio value, that would otherwise be done on your broker's server. That is significantly quicker than a traffic-laden overworked broker server doing the calculations then sending you the results by rebuilding a web page.

Consequently the active trader has instant price and chart data, thus avoiding costly decisions based on outdated information.

Why are active browsers faster in execution? And why does it matter?

The speed of trade execution is a second advantage of an active trader broker over a browser-based broker. With a browser-based broker your order goes via the internet to the server to be executed usually via third-party intermediaries. All this adds delays, sometimes more than 20 minutes, during which the price at which you buy or sell the stock can be far worse than you saw on screen originally. The difference between buying 1,000 shares at $100.00 and $100.50 is $500. If that net effect occurs only once a week it can represent more than $26,000 in annual hidden costs.

Active trader brokers save time and money by avoiding routing orders via third-party intermediaries and instead provide direct market access or electronic direct access trading (E-DAT).

What about streamlined order entry?

Many active trader brokers cater for the active internet trader by providing streamlined order entry. Browser-based brokers often ask for confirmation of your order. That adds valuable seconds to order execution and can be annoying when trading intensively throughout the day. The active trader broker removes such (cautionary) hurdles.

Do active browsers provide any significant advantages in the provision of market information?

Yes. A richer source of market information is a fourth advantage of the active trader broker. For instance, level II quotes not only give you the best bid-ask prices of a stock but also all the prices at which others are queuing to buy or sell the stock. Such information allows you to see the depth of interest in a stock and to formulate trading strategies accordingly – should you sell now before those 40,000 shares in a TMT are sold by Lehman Brothers?

> A richer source of market information is a fourth advantage of the active trader broker

Do active brokers provide any advanced features over browser-based brokers, apart from speed and accuracy?

Yes. Yet another advantage of the active trader broker is that they usually permit margin trading – lending money based on your portfolio holdings with which you can trade and hence leverage your position. Of course that can accentuate the downside, but such facilities are offered only to the experienced trader.

So what are the practicalities involved in opening an active broker account?

Active trader brokers include Carlin (**www.carlingroup. com**), Direct Access Traders (**www.directaccesstrader. co.uk**), Interactive Brokers (**www.interactivebrokers.com**), CyBerCorp (**www.cybercorp.com**) and Tradecast (**www. tradecast.com**).

The closest equivalent in the UK to the above US trading sites is MyBroker (**www.mybroker.com**) and trading using contracts for differences via GNI (**www.gni.co.uk**) and Deal4Free (**www.deal4free.com**).

Not all offer the same service and a visit to each site is essential. Some, such as Direct Access Traders, charge a monthly licence for the software, although there is often a 100 per cent refund if you do a minimum number of trades per month. Direct Access Traders refunds the $268 charge in months where you do more than 50 trades.

If I want to trade more actively, what other things should I be thinking about?

1. Infrastructure is an essential expense for the active trader. I occasionally trade intra-day – in futures – and find a dual flat-screen workstation with dual Pentium processors running on fault-tolerant Windows NT essential to avoid system crashes from data overload. Visit Dell (**www.dell.com**) for prices.

2. Beware, however, short-term trading can be very unprofitable, time-consuming and addictive. Consider Michael Hensley who lost $180,000 day trading and filed for bankruptcy only to comment in the *Chicago Tribune* that he planned to invest the $14,000 from the sale of his home in the markets!

3. Clearly, great skill and learning of strategies is required to actively trade. At one extreme is day trading – buying and selling stocks within the day through high-value quick trades. Education is key to success as an active trader. In the UK, courses on day trading and short-term trading are offered by Direct Access Traders (**www.directaccesstrader.co.uk**), providing five days' training for £995. Good educational sites giving details of strategies include (**www.careerdaytrader.com**), **www.daytraders.com**, **www.activetraders.net** and **www.tradehard.com**.

> Education is key to success as an active trader

What if I don't want to trade more actively?

You should still consider active broker accounts. While features such as speed of execution and level II quotes are less relevant for infrequent investors, commissions can be significantly lower than browser-based brokers. For instance, Interactive Brokers charges $0.01 per share with a $1 minimum. There are no other fees or charges, effectively making it commission-free trading. Fig 14.1 shows that there are very few days that make big returns, which is why Fig 14.2 shows few traders doing it well.

Figure 14.1 Distribution of daily S&P 500 returns, 1998–2000

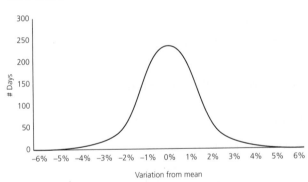

Source: DFA and Yahoo Finance

Since the big gains occur on only a few days, the argument goes that trying to time the market and be in the market on those days is like throwing dice and so one should not try to time the market. Of course we self-directed investors believe we can time the market, or can at least avoid some of the worst days.

Figure 14.2 A warning to equity investors – it isn't easy beating the market

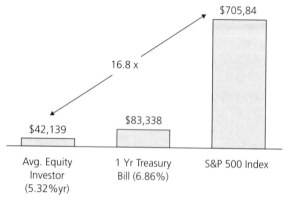

Avg. Equity Fund Investors vs T-Bill & S&P 500
Gain on $100,000 after Inflation (3.23%)
17 yrs – 1984–2000

Source: Dalbar, Inc., 2001, DFA

And Latin America sites?

Patagon

www.patagon.com

Patagon is a very comprehensive financial site. The site is widely used for expert opinions and real-time quotes on Latin American markets, essential for active traders. The site can be categorized as follows:

Its educational content has everything you need to know about the financial world explained in an instructive, easy and thorough manner. There are quote prices, official reports, and balances. Mergers, acquisition and takeover announcements, launching of new Latin American services and companies are included with data for the whole region. There is global news coverage with more than 400 daily wires and constant updates; in-depth market analysis with weekly guest speakers and individual company information; real-time discussion forums and an investment simulation game.

Latin Stocks

www.latinstocks.com

The Latin Stocks website is extremely extensive and broad since it covers breaking news from all the Latin American markets, focusing particularly on Argentina, Brazil and Mexico. In fact, there are separate country-specific set-ups of the basic Latin Stocks site:

www.latinstocks.com.ar (Argentina)
www.latinstocks.com.br (Brazil)
www.latinstocks.com.mx (Mexico)

All the Latin Stocks sites include various standard tools such as quick quotes, market indices, currency rates, interest rate, individual company snapshots, financial guides, S&P's analysis and mutual funds.

chapter fifteen

Why do so many people continue day trading? Is there something in it or not?

What is day trading?

When I buy shares, like most people I usually pay the offer price to buy them and the bid price to sell. The spread – that is the difference between the bid and offer prices – is pocketed by the market maker – the institutional individual on the other end of the deal.

A day trader tries to put himself in the position of the market maker by trying to buy stock at the (lower) bid price and sell it at the (higher) offer price through direct access to the market without using a broker but using special software and hardware from home or a trading booth at a day-trading firm. The day trader makes his money from this spread, although sometimes from any share price move as well.

Are there any problems with day trading?

> The main problem with day trading is that you are trying to make a profit from small price differences

The main problem with day trading is that you are trying to make a profit from small price differences. Take day-trading Amex stock standing at 1725 bid and 1728 ask. With $10,000 the day trader would buy 579 shares at 1725. Selling those at 1728 would realize merely $17.37 profit before costs.

Day traders require capital and time in abundance to make the activity worthwhile. First, they need a lot of capital to plough into the trade so that multiplied by the small price it results in an acceptable profit. Second, they need to trade a lot so that those small profits become something respectable, and that takes a lot of time.

Is it time-consuming?

Well, day traders have to be analyzing the market from open to close for those profitable opportunities. If you leave the screen for a few seconds the price could quickly move against you and since you are relying on small price moves from which to profit, it could easily result in a very large loss. Few people have the inclination to sit in front of a trading screen each day. You may be finished around 5 or 6 p.m., but what about the day job?

143

WHY DO SO MANY PEOPLE CONTINUE DAY TRADING? IS THERE SOMETHING IN IT OR NOT?

This is UK specific, but commissions are important. What are the commissions like?

Commissions are another excellent reason I do not day trade and why it will not be popular in the UK. A single £10,000 day trade (buying and selling) would cost £79.98 in commission. In the above example, even trading £40,000 worth of Barclay's stock would not overcome the commission, let alone provide enough money to live on or to compensate you for the time spent on the activity, and you would be buying at offer and selling at bid in any event, because online brokers do not provide direct market access.

Relatively high commissions in the UK compared with the US, where the above trade could cost $8 with Ameritrade (**www.ameritrade.com**), make the activity a good way to pay the brokers' wages and little else. Add 0.5 per cent stamp duty and that makes day trading in the UK even more unattractive.

Will I need any special technology to day trade?

Yes, and here lieth another dilemma. The unavailability of inexpensive technology makes day trading for private individuals very difficult. Day traders need level II quotes to trade effectively. Such quotes not only display the bid and the ask (level I) but also which firms have other orders at various prices. Such quotes are available in the US, but through software for your home PC or through specialist day-trading firms. And it is rare to find either available in the UK for the private investor. Reuters (**www.reuters.com**), Bloomberg (**www.bloomberg.com**) and Topic 3 (**www.primark.com**) screens are designed for and marketed to market professionals, not private traders – their lease costs run to more than $10,000 per annum.

Surely an ISDN connection is fast enough for day trading?

> **The internet is too slow for day trading**

The internet is too slow for day trading. A dedicated high-speed line (ISDN is too slow) is recommended by most advocates of the activity since day trading requires speed of reflex to capture small price moves, and to exit quickly in case larger price moves occur, thus magnifying losses. Such technology in the home does not come cheap and specialist day-trading firms providing it to private clients are not readily available.

Is day trading particularly a more difficult skill to acquire?

The skills required to be a day trader are yet another reason I dislike the activity. Looking for those small price moves, and knowing where and when to find them, while all the time the well-trained boys and girls from institutional banks like Lehman Brothers are also chasing them with state-of-the-art technology, places the odds definitely against the amateur, untrained individual.

What do the stats look like for day trading? Have investors been doing well day trading?

The North American Securities Association concluded a seven-month study recently and found that the high number of trades involved meant on average you needed to produce a 56 per cent annual return just to break even. The same study found 70 per cent of day traders lose money. The Securities and Exchange Commission (SEC) in the US found that in one firm 67 out of 68 day traders were losing money. These are definitely not my kind of odds. The SEC also estimates there are in any event only 5,000 day traders at most in the US. A lot of hoopla by a few over very little in my view.

The good thing about day trading is that, rather like poor gamblers at the roulette wheel, day traders remove themselves from the market anyway.

I'm still interested. Where can I find out more about day trading?

If you are still curious and want to find out more, visit Daypicks (**www.daypicks.com**), Trading Tactics (**www.tradingtactics.com**) or Elite Trader (**www.elitetrader.com**) for online chat about day trading and see Active Traders Network (**www.activetraders.net**) for more educational materials. For a UK perspective try **www.daytrader.co.uk**. Latin American Sites for day trading are, unfortunately, lacking.

Fig 15.1 illustrates that a few days account for greatest gains. This leads many to argue that the only sure way to capture those days is to always be in the market. Of course that also means capturing the bad days.

Others, most online traders included, try to capture the good days, accept that they will get a few mediocre days, and aim to exit quickly when it becomes clear they are in on a bad day.

Figure 15.1   S&P 500 index – distribution of monthly returns, January 1926 to June 2001

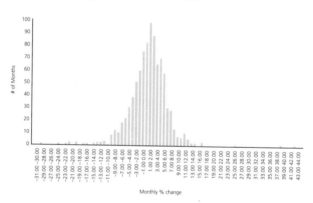

chapter sixteen

I want to trade actively, so what about options then?

A third of US online traders trade in options as well as stocks, according to a 1999 survey by TheStreet.com.

What are the advantages of options trading?

US options trading has many advantages – it makes more sense in terms of returns, it offers commissions savings, choice of securities, ease of market access, removes other hidden costs, quality options websites, and even free educational material.

Can you give me a definition of options?

In the complex version, an option is the right but not the obligation to buy or sell a given product at a fixed price (the exercise or strike price) before a predetermined date (the expiry date). The price at which that option trades (premium) depends on market supply and demand and theoretical pricing models incorporating variables such as the volatility of the product, time until the option expires, interest rates and other factors we need not worry about yet.

Aren't the mechanics of options trading quite complicated?

Yes, but simply stated, call options rise in value and put options fall in value if the underlying share price rises, all other things being equal. The reverse is true if the price falls.

So what are options used for?

> While there are sophisticated uses of options, many online options traders will use them as leveraged instruments for relatively short-term trades lasting at most a few months

While there are sophisticated uses of options, many online options traders will use them as leveraged instruments for relatively short-term trades lasting at most a few months.

Let's take a UK example, although the same principle applies in the US. You may buy the HSBC October 1600 option costing £2,360 per options contract. That would give you the right to buy 1000 HSBC shares at 1600p each by mid-October should you wish to exercise the right. If the share price rose 10 per cent in three weeks the option may then trade at 357p, i.e. if you sold the option you would make £3,570 – £2,360 = £1,210. A return of over 50 per cent on the option on a mere 10 per cent rise in the share price.

So why are such trades attractive?

There are many optionable securities, giving you lots of choice in selecting opportunities. If starved of choice, one has to either make second-best trades or simply not trade for prolonged periods. Inevitably trading performance improves.

What about commissions?

Typical big-name, reliable US e-brokers such as Ameritade (**www. ameritrade.com**) and Accutrade (**www.accutrade. com**) may charge around $25 for a single options contract.

> Education is essential for both the novice and intermediate-level options trader since the risks can be substantial

Should I trade index options?

Index options trade on the performance of a stock market index rather than a particular share. It can be a lot easier to have a view on a major index than a particular stock. After all, there is no shortage of analysis about the Nasdaq, Dow Jones, FTSE, etc. and their projected levels. How many commentators write as frequently about Pacific Media or Tadpole? Simplicity also stems from not having to analyze company reports, earnings estimates and accounts – although arguably predicting the Dow Jones direction is not made any easier despite the volume of commentary about it.

Ok, how do they work?

In the same way as share options. A 'call' option on the Dow Jones increases in price, all things being equal, as the Dow Jones rises. A 'put' option rises in price as the Dow Jones falls. Obviously a Dow Jones put option is a useful product in bear markets.

Can you give me an example?

As an example, let's take the FTSE 100. If the index stands at 6100, you feel that the market is going to rise and decide to buy two July 6200 call option contracts. The premium is quoted at 250 index points such that your outlay for two contracts is £5,000 (2 x 250 x £10) excluding dealing costs.

The index rises and stands at 6300 at the end of May. The July 6200 call option may then be quoted at 350 index points. Feeling that the stock market has peaked, you make a closing sale, realizing a profit of £2,000, excluding dealing costs.

Can I profit in a bear market?

Yes, index options are seen as attractive in that it is possible to profit from a falling market, thereby allowing – in theory at least – superior returns in a bear market or just having an insurance policy against the falling value of a stock portfolio.

> Yes, index options are seen as attractive in that it is possible to profit from a falling market

I hear options also provide greater leverage?

Options also provide leverage whereby limited capital can produce significantly greater gains than a similar amount invested in a single stock. For instance, a 5 per cent move in an index could mean more than 100 per cent return on the option.

Yes, but what are the difficulties of options trading?

Despite the benefits of trading index options, there are significant pitfalls because of their complexity. The leverage that options trading provides can produce a sharp loss as quickly as a profit. Because they are complex, investors often start trading them before they are fully qualified, not knowing which options provide the optimal performance, and consequently they often make basic, avoidable mistakes (such as buying the 'cheaper' options, which generally, however, expire worthless, or buying stock options – which will be discussed separately – in low volatility stocks).

How do I find out more about options?

Many more complexities are involved than the above examples reveal and the key to options success is intensive investor education – both for novice and inter-mediate-level traders since the risks can be substantial.

I recommend using the educational tools of web, software, books and training courses to fully understand the nomenclature of options, including essential terms such as in-the-money, butterfly spreads, delta, vega, gamma, and which trading strategies are the best for your particular risk profile.

The 1999 TheStreet.com survey revealed that already nearly one in three US online investors trade options. In my experience, options are misunderstood, perceived as highly risky and inaccessible for the private investor, partly because of a lack of awareness about the abundance of excellent educational material.

Which sources do you recommend?

The best books on options trading include Peter Temple's *Traded Options* and Michael Thomsett's *Getting Started in Options*. Remember to look for discounts on online bookstores such as **www.amazon.com**.

Exchanges provide a very good resource for learning about the operation of options. Visit **www.liffe.com** and the Chicago Board Options Exchange, **www.cboe.com**. Although the latter is American, the principles are the same. More usefully both exchanges provide ample free material on options and trading strategies, including software demonstrations of options principles. If in Chicago, the CBOE is worth a visit now that London does not have floor traders. Other excellent educational sites include Options Industry Counciil (**www.optionscentral. com**), Chicago Board of Trade (**www.cbot.com**) and Matrix Options (**www.matrixoptions.com**).

Option courses are offered by Training for Profit (**www.trainingforprofit.co.uk**), Stour Concepts (**www. stourconcepts.com**) and The Investors' Club (**www. investorsclub.co.uk**).

Useful US options sites providing quotes, strategies, commentary, discussion boards and hot options tips include the diverse INO Global Markets (**www.ino.com**), MoneyNet (**www.moneynet.com**) and the easy-to-use Financial Web (**www.financialweb.com**).

OK, this is complicated, so give me a textbook round-up for reference.

An option is a contract between the holder and the grantor (called **writer** of the option). A holder pays the writer a **premium** for entering into the contract. There are basically two types: **call** options and **put** options.

KEY TERMS

Writer
Strike price or exercise price
Exercise period or expiry date
Premium

Figure 16.1 Long call

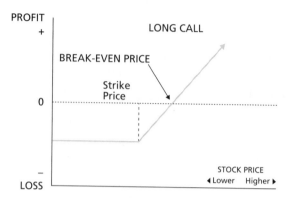

The X-axis represents the price level of an underlying stock.
The Y-axis represents profit and loss, above and below the
X-axis intersection respectively.

Figure 16.2 Long put

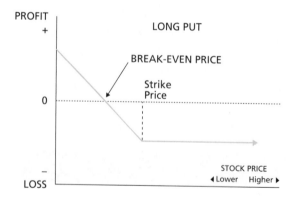

The X-axis represents the price level of an underlying stock.
The Y-axis represents profit and loss, above and below the
X-axis intersection respectively.

A call gives the holder the right, but not the obligation, to buy from the writer:

1. within a fixed period of time (the **exercise period);**

2. a fixed quantity of the underlying security;

3. at a fixed price (being the **exercise price** or **strike price**).

Example

In the UK, 'one contract of the Barclays July 1100 calls priced at 67p' would give the holder the right to buy, any time before a fixed date in July, from the writer 1,000 shares in Barclays Bank at a price of 1100 pence (or £11) each. To purchase the option in the first place the holder would have to pay the writer £670 (1,000 x 67 pence) as premium.

NOTA BENE

In the US equity options relate to the right to buy or sell 100 shares, and in the UK to 1000 shares.

Example

ABC Corp. July 80 calls entitle the holder to purchase 100 shares of ABC Corp. common stock at $80 per share at any time prior to the option's expiry in July.

What's the big idea 'ere?

Call holders therefore want the underlying share price to rise

The general idea is of course to make money! The flexibility of options (see below) provides many ways in which this can be done. One of the simplest ideas is (in the case of a call option holder) to buy shares in the future from the option writer at the fixed exercise price and then immediately sell them in the market at a profit, assuming the market price is greater than the exercise price. In the Barclays example, if the underlying price of the stock was 1200 at expiry in July, the holder would call for his 1,000 shares (at a cost of £11 each) and then sell them immediately in the market at £12 each. Call holders therefore want the underlying share price to rise.

NOTA BENE

Whether or not the option is exercised the writer keeps the premium

From the point of view of the writer or seller of the option, he is obliged if 'called' upon to sell the 1000 shares in Barclays Bank and would receive the £11 per share in return. The writer wants to profit from receiving his premium and not being forced to sell the holder any shares in the future. The call writer therefore does not generally want the market price to rise above the strike price, otherwise he will have to sell to the call holder at a lower price than he could get in the market. In the above example a call writer would have to sell at £11 under the option, when in the market he could otherwise have received £12. Call writers therefore do not want the underlying share price to rise.

> Call writers therefore do not want the underlying share price to rise

Similarly, a put option gives the holder the right, but not the obligation, for a fixed period of time to sell to the writer a fixed quantity of the underlying security at a fixed price.

Most people trade in **traded options**. That means they can sell the option contract itself to someone else if they so wish, without ever exercising it.

What about the strike price?

Each common stock will have numerous options with differing strike prices. The strike price for an option is initially set at a price which is reasonably close to the current share price. The exchange introduces other strike prices at fixed intervals from that initial strike price.

Read the press

Premiums for exchange traded options are often printed in major financial newspapers. Typically the listing may look as follows (only calls have been shown):

Option & closing price	Strike price	May	June	July
ABC	105	7 1/2	9 1/4	10 1/8
112 3/8	110	3	4 3/4	6 1/4
112 3/8	115	13/16	2 1/8	3 1/2
112 3/8	120	13/16	7/8	1 3/4
112 3/8	125	1/16	no option	13/16

In the above illustration, ABC May 115 calls are trading at 13/16 or $81.25.

How is the option price calculated and how can I profit?

The price at which an option is bought and sold is called the premium. In the Barclays example the option premium was 67p. This is a little like a margin payment.

An option's premium has two components, the **intrinsic value** and the **time value**.

Intrinsic value

A call option has intrinsic value if the underlying security price is greater than the option's strike price. A put option has intrinsic value if the underlying security price is less than the strike price.

KEY TERMS

Intrinsic value
(Share Price) < (Strike Price) = Put option has
intrinsic value

(Share Price) > (Strike Price) = Call option has intrinsic value

In-the-money option (An option with intrinsic value)

Out-of-the-money option (An option without intrinsic value)

So in our above example, if the price of Barclays' shares was 1110p, then the option's intrinsic value would be 10p. That is, if you exercised the call you could buy Barclays' shares from the writer at 1100p (strike price) and sell them in the market at 1110p (underlying security price). That is also why an option can never be worth less than its intrinsic value.

> **If an option has intrinsic value it is in-the-money. If an option has no intrinsic value it is out-of-the-money**

A call option would have no intrinsic value, and so only time value, if the underlying price was lower than the strike price. If an option has intrinsic value it is in-the-money. If an option has no intrinsic value it is out-of-the-money. An option whose strike price is nearest to the underlying price is at-the-money.

EXERCISES

(Share Price) < (Strike Price) = In-the-money put / Out-of-the-money call

(Share Price) > (Strike Price) = Out-of-the-money put / In-the-money call

Time value

The second component of option premium is time value. It is the difference between the option premium and its intrinsic value.

So in our previous example time value would total 57p. Time value essentially represents the price the holder pays the writer for the uncertainty. It is the cost of risk which the writer faces. Time value erodes as expiry approaches. Therefore an option is a wasting asset in the hands of the holder.

Time value can be calculated using complex mathematical option pricing models such as the Cox-Rubenstein Model. The variables are risk-free interest rates, strike price, underlying security volatility, underlying security price and any dividends which would be paid if the underlying security were held.

Figure 16.3   Time value = premium – intrinsic value

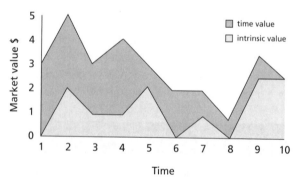

What are the factors affecting time value?

- Interest rates – higher interest rates tend to result in higher call premiums and lower put premiums
- Dividends – higher cash dividends imply lower call premiums and higher put premiums
- Volatility – volatility of the underlying stock places a greater risk on the writer that the stock will expire in-the-money and so volatility raises premium

From the above it follows that at expiry (when time value equals zero) an out-of-the money option is worthless and an in-the-money option is worth its intrinsic value. Note that since an option cannot have negative intrinsic or time value, the most an option holder can lose (and the most a writer can make) is the premium, no matter how much the underlying price changes.

What is the relationship between the option price and the price of the underlying security?

The most important thing to remember is that the price of a call tends to rise as the underlying security price rises and the price of a call tends to fall as the underlying security price falls. The price of a put tends to rise as the underlying security price falls and the price of a put tends to fall as the underlying security price rises.

So why buy an option and not the security? Because an option is leveraged. That means that for a given percentage change in the underlying price the option price can change by a greater percentage. You get a bigger bang for your buck.

Going back to our previous example, if the price of Barclays moved from 1110p to 1150p, the option price may move from 67p to 97p. That means there would have been a 3.6 per cent change in the underlying price and a 44.7 per cent change in the option price. You could then decide to sell the option or exercise it as before. There would be more money to be made from selling it.

The price of an option rarely has a 1:1 correlation with the underlying security price. The delta is the rate of change of the option price to the rate of change of the underlying price. So, for example, a delta of 0.5 means that if the underlying price rises by, say, 10 cents, then the option price will change by 5 cents. Obviously the greater the delta, the greater the bang for your buck. However, the delta is greatest for in-the-money options, i.e. those with the most intrinsic value and therefore the most costly options. Consequently, when calculating potential returns you have to draw a balance between the delta and the price of the option.

An example will clarify the situation. Barclays shares are trading at 1110p. July 1100 calls are 51p; July 1200 calls are 16p. If tomorrow the price of Barclays shares were to be 1200p then it may be that the July 1100 calls trade at 123p (average delta of 0.8) and the July 1200 calls trade at 22.5p (average delta of 0.25).

The return from the July 1100s is 141 per cent and only 41 per cent from the cheaper 1200s. Of course, in this example we have only estimated deltas and have ignored costs and bid-ask spreads. Nevertheless it gives you some idea of the balances that need to be drawn. For modest moves one is likely to profit most from just in-the-money options.

Can you give an example of leverage?

To own 100 shares of a stock trading at $30 per share would cost $3000. On the other hand, to own a $5 option with a strike price of $30 would give you the right to buy 100 shares for $30 at any time up to expiry. The option would cost only $500 ($5 x 100 shares).

If one month after the option is purchased the stock price has risen to $33, then the gain on the stock investment is $300, or 10 per cent. However, for the same stock increase the option may have increased to $7, for a return of $200 or 40 per cent.

Leverage of course has parallel downside implications. If in the above example the stock fell to $27, the loss on the stock investment would be $300 or 10%. For this $3 fall the option may now be worth $3 itself, i.e. a 40% loss.

Vive la différence

Options are in many respects similar to shares for the purposes of trading for profit.

Similarities

- Orders to buy and sell are handled by brokers
- Trading is conducted on regulated exchanges
- Pricing mechanisms are open and transparent
- Investors have the opportunity to follow price movements second by second if they wish

Differences

- Options have a limited life
- There are fewer options than stocks
- Option owners have no rights over a company; they are not shareholders
- Option holders receive no dividends

Where are the strategies?

Although there are only two types of option, calls and puts, there are a lot of option strategies. With options you can protect your stock holdings from a price decline, you can prepare to buy a stock at a lower price, you can increase income on your current stock holdings, you can participate in a large market move even if you are unsure beforehand which way the market is going to move, and of course you can participate in a stock rise or fall.

Kids' stuff

The simplest strategy is to go **long** a call or a put. That means you **buy to open** a call or put. If you go **short** (write the option) then you **sell to open** a call or put. In the latter case you have to post margin since your losses are potentially unlimited. It is a lot safer for the lay investor to be long puts than short calls even though on both you profit from falling prices. A common options strategy already discussed above is to purchase calls to participate in an upward price movement.

Locking in a price

Another popular use of calls is to lock in an attractive stock purchase price. Imagine that ABC is trading at $55 and you believe they are about to increase in value but you do not have the funds to buy 100 shares. You know you will have the funds in six months, but you are afraid that if you wait that long the shares will increase in value.

You see that the option expiring eight months hence at the strike price of $55 costs $3, i.e. $300. If you buy one contract and then in six months the price of the stock is

$70, you could exercise your option and buy the stock for $5,500 + $300. Whereas if you did not have the option and had to buy the option in the open market, it would have cost you $7,000. So you just made a saving of $1200.

Puts to protect unrealized profit in a stock position

Imagine you bought ABC stock at $50 and it is now trading at $70. You fear there may be a short-term fall in the price but do not want to sell your holding on the hunch. By buying an ABC put option with a strike of $70 for $2 you are assured of being able to sell your stock at $70 no matter what happens to the stock price. If the price does not collapse, you will have lost the premium $2 x 100 = $200. Consider it an insurance premium.

But if the stock had fallen to, say, $55, you could have sold it at $70 per share, less $2 per share for the option premium. That means you would have earned an extra $13 per share with the option than if you had not taken out the insurance policy.

Option strategies are beyond the scope of this book but I will mention a few to give you some idea of what the professionals and the experienced non-professional can do with options.

- Hedge: a hedge is a position where one position profits if the other position loses. So a hedge can be thought of as an insurance against being wrong. For example, a hedge against a long call, one could sell short a different call or go long a put.

- Straddle: buy to open an at-the-money call and buy to open an at-the-money put. You profit by increased volatility in the underlying price irrespective of direction. The strategy is a **guts** if the options are both in-the-money and a **strangle** if they are both out-of-the-money.

■ Bull call spread: long in-the-money call and short out-of-the-money call. Profit from upward price movement. This becomes a **bull call calendar spread** if the short call is nearer month than the long call.

■ Bear put spread: long in-the-money put and short out-of-the-money put. Profit from downward price movement. This becomes a **bear put calendar spread** if the short put is nearer month than the long put.

Various other strategies exist depending on your views as to volatility and direction, and the extent of risk you wish to take. These strategies have some unusual names, such as butterfly, condor, iron butterfly (buy a straddle and sell a strangle because you expect a limited size move), combo, ladder, box, conversion and reversal.

Foreign trading

chapter seventeen

I want to trade foreign stocks – am I mad or ahead of the pack?

I am interested in foreign stocks. What do you recommend I do?

Why should we miss out on owning some world-beating stocks producing exceptional returns just because we do not have the tens of thousands of pounds often needed for a private client account with a major investment bank that would allow us to access global markets? Online trading allows us to trade foreign stocks cheaply, efficiently, quickly and easily through American depositary receipts (ADRs).

> Online trading allows us to trade foreign stocks cheaply, efficiently, quickly and easily

What are ADRs?

ADRs are dollar-denominated US securities backed by and related to the underlying company stock, which may, for instance, be UK-listed shares. The price of the ADR and the underlying stock will generally move in tandem. A complete list of ADRs is available on the excellent **www.global-investor.com**.

Why are ADRs more advantageous than direct trading?

Of course, in place of trading ADRs we could always open multiple foreign online trading accounts with different brokers, holding them in different currencies (facing conversion costs) and of course learn the language of each country since their e-broking sites often are not in English. Try E*Trade Korea (**www.etrade.co.kr**) for a taster of the difficulties.

> The efficient solution then becomes ADRs

What about tax – urghhhhh?

We can also face the problems of double taxation on our gains in those companies. For instance, the Korean government has rules about how much currency you can convert from sterling to local currency and how long you have to keep it in the country. In any event, do you know of a cheap online broker through which you can buy Telecomunicacoes Brasileiras 100 per cent in the past 18 weeks? The efficient solution then becomes ADRs, which avoid all of these difficulties.

Why should I trade in foreign stocks at all?

The reasons for trading in foreign stocks are compelling.

- First, other global regions may be experiencing superior growth rates to our own economy. Trading their stocks could significantly improve our performance. When the recession comes we may be able to avoid a downturn in our own performance by tapping into the economic cycle of a country or region going through a growth phase of its economic cycle. As one Salomon Smith Barney analyst commented about Latin America: 'The region enjoys unique characteristics that could turn it into the hottest internet market in the world.' Now, through ADRs I can act and profit from that analysis.

> ADRs are a compelling proposition that provides me with a wider selection of companies from which to choose the very best

- Second, I can have a more diversified portfolio exposed to a whole industry group I may find exciting but which is global rather than local. For instance, if I am interested in the telecoms sector, and in particular the telecoms equipment and wireless telephony industries, ADRs allow me to take advantage of better growth affecting the whole industry by not being restricted to only US companies in the field.

■ The third reason I find ADRs a compelling proposition is that they provide me with a wider selection of companies from which to choose the very best. The wider the choice, the greater the chance I will pick winners assuming my research remains diligent.

Are there any more advantages to ADRs?

> You pay US online trading commissions, which can be very low, even compared with those of brokers in other developed markets

A further advantage of trading ADRs is that they are traded like any other US security. You are only holding dollars, not numerous other currencies. You pay US online trading commissions, which can be very low, even compared with those of brokers in other developed markets like the UK.

Is there any special risk to trading in ADRs?

If you are residing in the UK, for example, trading UK stocks only, investing in ADRs for emerging markets will of course mean that you need to open an account offering US stock trading (with a UK or US broker). And here, with the ADR you have the currency risk of holding dollars and the conversion costs involved. But if you intend to put away for several months a pool of money for trading in dollar stocks and don't intend to convert back and forth, those costs and risks can be minimized.

What are the practicalities of trading ADRs?

Trading ADRs is straightforward. It is just like trading any US security. You would use a US e-broking account as you would for trading in, say, Microsoft or Intel. Which online broker should you use for trading ADRs? The same you use for your US stock trading, and if you don't have one yet then I usually recommend Ameritrade (**www.ameritrade. com**) or Datek (**www.datek.com**) because of positive personal experience and good feedback about them from others.

For the Brits, UK-based brokers also offer US stock trading. Popular ones include Schwab (**www.schwab-europe.com**). For a list of UK-based brokers offering US stock trading, visit the quaint but useful and informative GoShare site (**www. goshare.fsnet. co.uk**).

Any other sites for ADR investors?

Sites for the ADR investor include Global Investor (**www.global-investor.com**), and the content-rich Worldly Investor (**www.worldlyinvestor.com**), which offers a gob-smacking site with excellent columns to get the best ideas for the various regions you are interested in. Use the ADR stock screener to generate ideas of ADRs, although it is a bit basic. Sign up for the various free e-mail newsletters according to sector and region, e.g. Internet Europe. There is also the professional **www.adr.com** by J.P. Morgan as well as the Yahoo!Finance sites for each region, although these are not always in English (**www.yahoo.com**).

Latin America

If Latin America is of special interest to you, all of the following should be very useful.

Bescos **

www.bescos.com

A well-designed site with news, a summary of how the major indices are performing, news, commentary, a chat site plus excellent educational material. The size is clear, crisp and friendly to use.

Bloomberg Latin America **

www.bloomberg.com/sa

This site is quite general and offers only basic information about the major Latin American indices and financial news. Not as focused as some of the other sites.

Bloomberg TV ***

www.bloomberg.com

Watch live financial TV in Spanish from Bloomberg TV via the internet – excellent.

BradyNet **

www.bradynet.com

This site provides specific information on Mexico, Ecuador, Argentina, Venezuela and Brazil. There are market commentaries, a research library and individual company profiles. Charting and technical analysis is informative, but available only once you have registered.

Elpais **

www.elpais.es

This website for the popular paper is a good source of Spanish-specific content, as you would expect.

Expansion directo ***

www.expansion.recoletos.es

This site is very well designed. Use it for financial news and analysis and to stay on top of what is happening in the markets. It also has a useful archives section and online chat. The site includes news about companies, markets, finance, technology and Latin America.

Expansion Financiera *

www.expansion-financiera.com

The site is too bare. Should contain lots more information rather than one or two video clips.

Ganar.com **

www.ganar.com

Use this one for market news, as well as analytical commentary on technology and finance.

Latin Focus ***

www.latin-focus.com

Sharp, top-notch site. Just click on a nation and pull up a detailed economic profile. It is an excellent place for initial research.

LatinInvestor ***

www.latinvestor.com

The site has a wide range of authoritative reports from brokers and consulting firms on the major Latin American economies, companies and industries. Key market information is available on Argentina, Brazil, Chile, Mexico, Peru and Venezuela. However, only a small number of these reports are free.

Latin Stocks ***

www.latinstocks.com

The Latin Stocks website is extremely extensive and broad since it covers breaking news from all the Latin American markets, focusing particularly on Argentina, Brazil and Mexico. In fact, there are separate country-specific set-ups of the basic Latin Stocks site:

- **www.latinstocks.com.ar** (Argentina)
- **www.latinstocks.com.br** (Brazil)
- **www.latinstocks.com.mx** (Mexico)

All the Latin Stocks sites include various standard tools such as quick quotes, market indices, currency rates, interest rates, individual company snapshots, financial guides, S&P's analysis and mutual funds. The sites also include further excellent items: a free newsletter, a discussion forum and market chat. Analysis, assessment and standpoints are insightful. The sites have clear menus and are easy to navigate. Overall, these are well-designed and comprehensive sites.

MegaBolsa **

www.megabolsa.com

Use the site's educational material for an introduction to technical analysis. It has a host of news links, and analysis of the major Latin and Spanish markets.

Patagon ***

www.patagon.com

Patagon is a comprehensive financial site, widely used for expert opinions and real-time quotes on Latin American markets. The site can be categorized as follows:

- home page – gain access to a wide array of financial options, bank services and products;

- education – everything you need to know about the financial world explained in an instructive, easy and thorough manner;

- quotes, graphs and info – quote prices, official reports, balances. Mergers, acquisition and takeover announcements, launching of new Latin American services and companies. Data for the whole region;

- trading – buy and sell stocks, bonds and funds;
- news – global coverage with more than 400 daily wires. Constant updates;
- market analysis – in-depth analysis with weekly guest speakers and individual company information;
- community – real-time discussion forums. There is an investment simulation game.

Patagon is very broad. It provides a good starting point for newcomers through the educational and community section. Yet there is enough coverage of the major markets and sophistication in the analysis for the more experienced investor.

Senda Financiera *

www.sendafinanciera.com

Use this one to find the detailed technical analysis on the Ibex plus some stocks, market commentary and stock charts.

Yahoo!Finanzas Espana ***

http://es.finance.yahoo.com

Yahoo's own financial portal is useful for quotes on major European indices as well as news wires. Use it to get stock quotes, too. The news sources are quite exhaustive, including Reuters. A good one-stop shop.

ZonaFinanciera.com ***

www.zonafinanciera.com

What makes this site particularly useful is that it is very broad in terms of the number of countries it covers. The site offers separate, detailed information for all the major Latin American markets: Argentina, Bolivia, Brazil, Chile, Colombia, Costa Rica, Ecuador, El Salvador, Spain, Guatemala, Honduras, Mexico, Nicaragua, Panama, Paraguay, Peru, Puerto Rico, the Dominican Republic, Uruguay and Venezuela.

For each country, it is easy to find the most data on the markets, banks, insurance and real estate. Under the stocks section there is a complete review of the main developments in the markets and you can trade online in stocks and mutual funds. Market commentary is knowledgeable.

Alongside key indicators such as quick quotes, indices, currency and news reports, there is an interesting section, 'Investor School', that provides information on the basics as well as on strategic investing.

Any other relevant financial sites

Argentina

■ Mercantil Valores – stockbroker daily closing Buenos Aires SE stock prices and index levels (**www.totalnet.com.ar/Mercval**).

■ Ministry of Economy and Public Works and Services – quarterly economic report, etc. (**www.mecon.ar**).

■ National Statistics Institute – Spanish (**wewww.index.mecon.ar**).

Brazil

- Jornal do Brasil – (Portuguese) daily general/economic news (**www.jp.com.br**).
- Agencia Estado – (Portuguese) daily financial news (**www.agestado.com.br**).
- O Estado de S. Paulo – (Portuguese and English digest) daily news (**www.estado.com.br**).
- Banco da Bahia – (investment bank) daily reports with updated charts from the IBOVESPA and interest rates, inflation indices, future prices, daily stock report with closing prices (**www.bahiabank.com.br**).
- Sao Paulo SE – BOVSPA daily market reports, closing share prices (**www.bovespa.com.br**).

Chile

- Chip News – daily news (**www.chip.cl**).
- Santiago SE – daily market summary: share indices, volume, major price movers (**www.bolsantiago.co**).
- Bolsa Electronica de Chile – (Spanish) real-time index charts (**www.bolchile.cl**).
- Chilean Govt Network (**www.presidencia.cl**).
- Banco Central de Chile – Spanish (**www.bcentral.cl**).

Portugal

- Publico Online – (Portuguese) full text of daily newspaper (**www.publico.pt/publico/hoje**).
- The News – English (**www.nexus-pt.com**).

- Lisbon SE – BVL30 stock index updated every five minutes (**www.bvl.pt**).
- ICEP – brief economic overview (**www.portugal.org**).

Spain

- Banesto – weekly market comment, analysis on stocks (**www.banesto.es**).
- Fincorp – daily exchange rates, money and bond rates, stock indices, brief market news (**www.servicom.es/fincorp**).
- Madrid SE – (**www.bolsamadrid.es**).
- Stock Research – (Spanish) technical analysis newsletter (**www.meff.es**).
- BBV – monthly economic report (**www.bbv.es**).

chapter eighteen

What about riskier foreign markets then?

How can I be truly global in my trading?

Well, thanks to the internet it is easier to trade stocks in emerging markets, from Eastern Europe to Israel, South Africa to Asia, and Latin America. A wave of online brokers and websites is available to help research, buy and monitor such stocks.

Do emerging markets perform well?

Advocates of emerging markets argue the performances of some of the national stock indices speak for themselves. After all, the world's best performing stock market last year was an emerging market, the Shanghai B Index, which rose 136 per cent.

But those types of gains in your portfolio are elusive. To start with, historic performance is a poor indicator of future returns whatever the market. India's Sensex rose around 80 per cent in 1999, only to fall 25 per cent during the next 12 months.

> Emerging markets have no monopoly on strong gains, either

Emerging markets have no monopoly on strong gains, either. And if you do pick a country whose stock exchange rises over the year, you'll still need to choose the right stocks. Mexico's Inmex index could be up 15 per cent this year, but within that index Telefonos de Mexico could be down 33 per cent.

How can I find out about the performance of emerging markets myself?

Try excellent emerging markets sites like **www.worldly investor.com**, **www.mfinance.com**, **www.latinfocus.com** and **www.global-investor.com**.

So if the past performance of emerging markets isn't a good enough reason to invest, maybe their potential is?

The advocates argue that these regions have so much growth potential that their companies should grow far faster than companies in more mature western economies.

Take China's telecoms sector, which is often portrayed as the perfect example of why you should invest in emerging markets. Every month, there are two million new telephone lines being installed and over two million mobile phone subscriptions bought. The potential for further growth is huge because 75 per cent of China's population have never made a phone call.

> These regions have so much growth potential that their companies should grow far faster than companies in more mature western economies

So, if the potential reward is so huge, should I invest in China Mobile, the world's third largest mobile phone company, or China Unicom, the country's only fully integrated telecoms company?

The answer is neither. Just because an emerging market has potential doesn't mean its own stocks are the best investment to reap that potential. Nor does it mean that stocks in developed markets lack potential and if the potential argument does not work for Chinese telecoms, it seems even more unconvincing for other sectors, let alone emerging markets with a smaller population to exploit for growth.

I would far rather tap into the potential of emerging markets through investing in long-established Western multinationals that are doing deals in the region. For instance, in 2000 Vodafone paid £648 million for a stake in the Mexican mobile company Grupo Iusacell. If the region delivers

I would far rather tap into the potential of emerging markets through investing in long-established Western multi-nationals that are doing deals in the region

extraordinary growth, Vodafone's share price will reflect that; if not, then at least Vodafone's European and US businesses (which yield the bulk of its £1.3 billion profits) will cushion any blow to the share price. Besides, can the local emerging markets companies claim to be successful in the fierce developed markets and use that knowledge and power locally?

How do I buy stocks in emerging markets?

If you still wish to buy stocks in emerging markets, the internet offers three approaches:

- First, through online brokers such as the comprehensive Brunswick Direct (**www.brunswickdirect.com**) which provides access to 26 emerging markets.

- Second, there is the depository receipts route (ADRs and GDRs – global depository receipts). These are tradable securities (denominated in dollars) based on the underlying shares of non-US companies. They are traded through the same brokers used to trade US stocks, for instance **www.eschwab.com**.

- Third, there are pooled investments. To find which unit trusts and investment trusts invest in emerging markets and their historic performance, visit **www.trustnet.com**.

As with much on the internet, just because the opportunity is there doesn't mean you should take it. And more so with emerging markets, which always seem to be emerging but never quite arriving.

Figure 18.1 Significant events, 1941–91

Date	Event
1/17/91	US launches bombing attack on Iraq
8/2/90	Iraq invades Kuwait
3/30/81	President Reagan shot
8/9/74	President Nixon resigns
11/22/63	President Kennedy assassinated
10/22/62	Cuban Missile Crisis
9/26/55	President Eisenhower heart attack
6/25/50	North Korea invades South Korea
12/7/41	Japan attacks Pearl Harbor, Hawaii

Figure 18.2 Growth of a dollar, August 1926 to July 2001

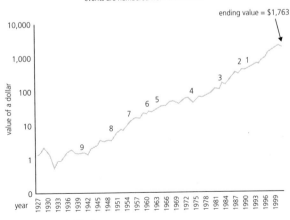

Growth of a Dollar (log plot) Aug 1926 to July 2001
Center for Research on Security Prices, Total Market Index
events are numbered from table above

Source: **www.ifa.tv**

Even through crisis, the dollar keeps getting stronger – a good argument for holding dollar-denominated shares and not foreign ones in the long term.

chapter nineteen

How does foreign exchange affect my portfolio?

How do exchange rates affect my foreign stock?

Calculate!

The value of the exchange rate will obviously affect the value of your foreign stock. As the exchange rate of the dollar appreciates (depreciates), the price of foreign stock in dollars will fall (rise), before taxes and fees and not accounting for dividends.

Fill in the template below for a share of your choice.

Exchange rate to $1 at purchase	_____	(A)
Exchange rate to $1 now	_____	(B)
Share price at purchase	$_____	(C)
Shares purchased	_____	(D)
Share price today	$_____	(E)

The stock price now unadjusted for the exchange rate is (E). The stock price now adjusted for the exchange rate variation that took place over the period between purchase of the stock and now is:

$$E * \{1 - [(B - A) / A]\} = \rule{2cm}{0.4pt} = G$$

Call the above figure G. The gain per share will therefore be:

$$G - C = \rule{2cm}{0.4pt}$$

At the original exchange rate of A, your return would be:

$$(E - C) / C = \rule{2cm}{0.4pt}$$

Given the new rate of exchange of B, your return would be:

$$(G - C)/C = \rule{2cm}{0.4pt}$$

Explanation?

When the amount of the foreign currency required to be exchanged for $1 increases (the dollar appreciates), your profits on an investment decrease if you sell. If the amount required decreases, your profits increase. In other words, when the dollar becomes more valuable, your return decreases. If the dollar weakens in relation to the foreign currency, your return increases (Figs 19.1 and 19.2).

If the dollar weakens and the foreign currency becomes more valuable, the value of your foreign stock increases.

The lesson

If you want to invest in companies traded on foreign stock exchanges, you'll need to consider foreign exchange rates.

Figure 19.1 Price vs future exchange rate

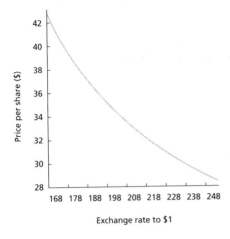

Figure 19.2 Rate of return vs exchange rate

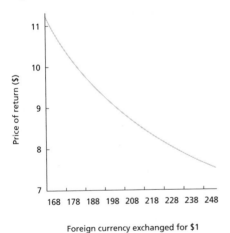

Foreign exchange refers to the conversion of money of one country into its equivalent in the currency of another country. Exchange rates fluctuate daily, making your investment in, say, a France or India-based stock worth more or less, depending on the relative values of the French franc or the Indian rupee versus the US dollar.

How much do fees affect my rate of return?

Calculate!

Note: here we are excluding dividends and taxes, which would have an effect on the result.

Share price at purchase $_____ (A)

Shares purchased   _____ (B)

Share price today $_____ (C)

	Fees at purchase	Fees at sale
As fixed dollar amount	$_____ (D)	$_____ (E)
As % of total amount	_____% (F)	_____% (G)
As dollar amount per share	$_____ (H)	$_____ (I)

Your total gain without fees would be

$(A*B) - (C*B)$ = _____

Your total gain with fees would be:

$$[\{(B * [A + H]) * [(F / 100) + 1]\} + D] - [\{(B * [C - I]) * [1 - (G / 100)]\} - E]$$

= _____

(Don't let the formula intimidate you; a lot of the entries will be zero because you will not be assaulted with a fee at every stage.)

Explanation?

When you pay a fee may be as important as the amount you pay. The chart below gives you a rough idea of the number of percentage points your rate of return drops due to the amount and type of fees you may pay.

Fees can be more damaging, all things being equal, when they are placed upfront on your principal, rather than in arrears (Fig. 19.3).

Figure 19.3 Comparison of fees paid upfront against fees paid at sale

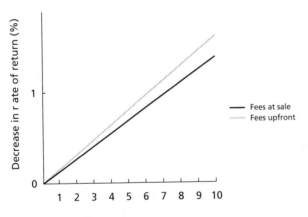

Fees as per cent of total amount (%)

The lesson

Transaction fees, mostly in the form of brokerage commissions, lower your rate of return on a stock investment.

What is my current yield from dividends?

Calculate!

Share price today	$_____	(A)
Shares owned	_____	(B)
Average quarterly dividend	$_____	(C)

The current yield on your dividend as a percentage is (before tax):

$\{[C * 4] / [A * B]\} * 100 =$ _____

Explanation?

Dividend yield is simply the dollar amount of dividends you receive in a 12-month period from an investment, divided by the current market value of the investment.

The lesson

Dividend yields for most large-cap stocks have diminished to well below 3 per cent. Note also that the dividend income is taxed as ordinary income, which lowers your after-tax return.

Which are better: income or growth stocks?

Calculation has not been included in this section because the question is quite general and the calculation would be

too complicated to work out on paper … lucky for you!
Nevertheless, here's an explanation.

Explanation?

Growth stocks are those stocks that pay little or no
dividends in exchange for a larger expected appreciation in
share price. Income stocks, on the other hand, pay steady
and growing dividends in exchange for a smaller expected
appreciation in share price.

The annualized rate of return on a stock investment is
calculated using the following two methods:

■ Internal rate of return (IRR). With IRR, any cash
  dividends are assumed to be reinvested in additional
  shares of the stock.

■ Financial management rate of return (FMRR). FMRR
  assumes that dividends are invested in a money
  market account.

The lesson

When comparing growth and income stock, the return on
a growth stock will rise much faster with a rise in the
selling price per share than it would for an income stock
(because most of the return on an income stock is accrued
from dividend and earnings).

Figure 19.4 below gives you a rough idea that as the
share price increases, growth stocks would be more advan-
tageous. The problem, however, is knowing whether the
share price will rise. In a bear market, income stocks would
look like a better investment if held for a while. As the
figure suggests, higher price volatility would mean that the
return on growth stocks would fluctuate more markedly

than income stock (which would receive more stable dividends earnings). Therefore if you are quite risk averse or the market particularly volatile, you may be better off in income stocks.

Figure 19.4 Comparison of growth and income stocks based on price changes

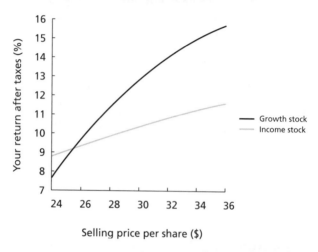

EXERCISES

1. What is an exchange rate?

2. What is the relationship between the exchange rate of the dollar to price per share and to the rate of return of foreign stock?

3. What are dividends?

4. What is current dividend yield?

5. What is an income stock?

Suggested answers

1. Basically, it is the amount of foreign currency required to buy one unit of home currency (let's assume the US is home). It is the value of home currency (dollar) in terms of foreign currency. If more foreign currency is required to buy $1, the exchange rate has appreciated and the value of the dollar has risen.

2. As the value of the dollar exchange rate appreciates relative to, say, sterling, the price of stock in UK firms and so the return on that stock must fall. A strong dollar can mean investment in stock abroad has become less attractive.

3. Dividends are the distributions of cash or securities to a company's shareholders that have been declared by a company's board of directors. They are usually expressed as 'per share'. US companies that pay dividends usually do so four times a year. For example, 100 shares of a stock paying a dividend of $2.75 per share generate $275 in dividends.

4. The annual dollar interest paid by a share or bond divided by its market price. Current yield is a measure of part of the rate of return on the investment.

5. An income stock is a stock that has very low share price volatility and the share price tends to have a low expected appreciation (as opposed to a growth stock); rather, income stocks have larger dividend payments.

Finale

chapter twenty

Am I better off not trading online? Surely not?

Is there anyone left in the US who does not have an e-brokerage account or at least know someone who has one?

Online trading looks set to become as mainstream as having a mortgage, but far more fun, of course. However, dangers lurk for the converts from offline trading which hitherto have hardly been mentioned. An academic study by Brad Barber, author of stock research from the University of California at Santa Barbara, reveals some intriguing findings no online trader can afford to ignore.

So, what are the dangers?

Commissions would appear to be a good reason to trade online. It seems obvious that if commissions on the whole are lower online, then one would definitely be better off online.

How are low commissions a danger?

Well, according to the Barber study it appears that those trading offline tend to beat the market by about 2 per cent per annum, yet when they go online they suffer in their returns – lagging the market by 3 per cent annually. This despite lower commission costs.

So what is the cause?

One major cause of the fall-off in performance is that in going online, traders tend to trade more actively. It is easy to see why that would be so.

- First, lower costs remove the obstacle of concern about whether 'the trade is really justified'.
- Second, with faster execution speeds and ease of access to one's account through the internet at any time, and especially the real-time update of one's portfolio, it is not difficult to see why people would want to 'fiddle' with the stocks owned, buy the next hot thing, or just chase the market.

How do I remedy the problem of overtrading?

The advice I would give to online traders in such a position is to clearly plan why a particular trade is worth placing, what they expect the stock to do and why, over what time frame, and to set exit levels. In the words of Bill Lipschutz, former global head of foreign exchange at Salomon Brothers, taken from *The Mind of a Trader*: 'In a year you might place 250 trades. In the end it comes down to five. On three you lose a fortune and on two you make more of a fortune.' The point is to be patient and to pick your trades with good reason.

But there is more to poor online trading performance than simple overtrading due to low costs. The source of the overtrading is apparently psychological and rooted in overconfidence.

What causes this sudden burst of self-confidence, and what can we online traders do to protect against it and so also protect our returns?

According to psychologists, humans have a tendency to be overconfident in their own abilities and their knowledge. They tend to attribute any success to their own abilities even when that is not warranted.

> 'Don't mistake a bull market for skill.'

Remember the old market saying: 'Don't mistake a bull market for skill.'

But there is so much information on the net, surely I can't go wrong?

The availability of information, of which there is an abundance online, also leads to overconfidence. Consider the quantity and quality of information on sites such as **www.ft.com**, **www.bloomberg.co.uk** and **http://finance. uk.yahoo.com**.

> They have the illusion of knowledge

The more information you give someone, the more *over*-confident they are likely to become. They have the illusion of knowledge. The illusion of knowledge leads to the illusion of control for the online trader. Overconfidence leads to more speculative trading without proper detailed analysis and that leads to greater losses and worse online trading performance.

Would-be and existing online traders therefore need to be aware of this problem and to find ways of challenging it to improve their performance.

So some tips then?

- **Risk management:** on a detailed analysis of the stock you plan to trade in, is the upside potential greater than the downside risk by a ratio of at least 2:1? If for instance you bought 100 shares of XYZ at $50, expecting a rise to $60, it would not be wise to say you will stay with the trade even if the stock hits $25. In other words, how high do you expect it to go, and how low could it go before you knew it was not going to turn around and you had better exit?

- **Objectivity:** maintaining an objective view about a trade is essential to being able to exit without 'psychological' difficulties. Do not become attached to a stock. The key issue is one of probability – is the expected gain on the upside greater than that on the downside?

- **Stop-losses:** have you set an exact price level at which you are not willing to accept further losses and will exit? This stop-loss cannot be too close to the price where you entered your position, otherwise even a small down move may trigger your stop-loss and cause you to exit. On the other hand, it cannot be too far from your entry price level otherwise you may lose all your investment before deciding to exit.

> Having formed a trading plan, stick to it!

- **Discipline:** having formed a trading plan, stick to it! It is surprising how many traders ignore their exit levels when the time comes to pull the trigger because their mind comes up with a hundred reasons not to exit.

There is another reason not to assume online trading is without downside. In Germany, online trading comes with a spiritual health warning. Evangelical churches there are concerned about the massive growth in online trading in search of quick profits. In my experience there is no conflict between online trading and spirituality – most online traders pray like crazy.

Glossary

Abandoned option Where an option is neither sold nor exercised but allowed to lapse at expiry.

Accumulation A technical analysis term describing a stock whose price is moving sideways.

Acid test ratio A measure of financial strength. Also known as the quick ratio. Cash plus short-term investments plus accounts receivable divided by current liabilities for the same period. All other things being equal, a relatively high figure may indicate a healthy company.

Active channels A feature of Internet Explorer 4. Internet sites that are selected as channels provide special IE4 content. Bill Gates wants to lead internet TV, hence the term channels.

Active market Securities trading with a relatively high degree of liquidity, the major benefit of which is narrow spreads. A term of art rather then precision.

Aftermarket Also known as 'secondary market', referring to the trading in a security after its initial public offering.

All or none Order instructing the broker to buy or sell the entire amount of the order in one transaction or not at all.

American depositary receipt (ADR) Effectively like owning in dollars stocks of US-listed companies. A popular form of owning shares of foreign companies.

American option An option that is exercisable at any time within its life. Can be traded outside Europe and are.

American Stock Exchange (AMEX) Located in New York, this is the third-largest US stock exchange. Shares trade in the same 'auction' manner used by the larger New York Stock Exchange unlike the Nasdaq's 'market-making' methods.

Arbitrage The purchase in one market of an instrument and the sale in another market of it or a closely linked instrument in order to profit from the small price differentials between the products in the two markets. Arbitrage profits usually exist only for a short time because someone usually swoops on them since they are 'locked in'.

Arbitrageur A trader engaged in arbitrage. They seek to make a lot of small, quick profits.

Ask The lowest price at which a dealer or market maker will sell a security (also, 'bid', 'offer').

Assign To oblige a call option writer to sell shares to the option holder, or to oblige a put option writer to buy shares from a put option holder.

At the close Order instructing to be filled as close as possible to the market close.

At the market An order to buy or sell at the best price obtainable in the market.

At the open Order instructing the transaction to be filled in one of the first trades for a particular security, or to be cancelled otherwise.

Averaging Where a price moves against a trader and he trades more of the stock to enlarge his position but to lower his overall entry price. It will mean he will have a lower exit price at which he can make a profit.

Away from the market Trade orders that cannot be executed because they are above or below the current bid or ask. For example, a limit order to buy 50 shares of AOL at $105 when the best offer is $109 will not be filled and is said to be 'away from the market'.

Backbone A high-speed connection within a network that connects all the other circuits. Another name for a 'hub'. A central connection from which 'spokes' or connections radiate.

Bandwidth The capacity of a network to carry data. If your pipes are clogged (low bandwidth) then things take for ever to load. It's an issue not of length but of width.

Basis point Used to calculate differences in interest rate yields, e.g. the difference between 5.25 per cent and 6.00 per cent is 75 basis points.

BBS A bulletin board system. A little like an electronic notice board. You 'post' messages to the board and everyone who subscribes to the board can view them.

Bear(ish) An individual who thinks prices will fall.

Bear market A market in which prices are falling.

Bear spread An option position where it is intended to profit from a falling market. Usually the position involves the purchase of a put at one strike price and the sale of a put at a lower strike price.

Beta This measures the stock's volatility to the market as a whole. A beta value greater than 1.0 represents greater volatility than the general market; less than 1.0 represents less volatility than the general market.

Bid An offer to purchase at a specific price.

Big Board Nickname for the New York Stock Exchange. Greatly adds to your smugability if you only ever refer to the NYSE as the Big Board. The ignorant will instantly fall admiringly at your feet. That a person of flesh and blood could know so much!?

Black-Scholes Pricing Modelability A mathematical model used to calculate the price in theory of an option. The main input variables are: the risk-free interest rate, volatility, dividends, time to expiry, the strike price, underlying price.

Block As in 'the sale of a block of shares'. A transaction involving a large number of shares or other security. Often blocks are bought or sold at a discount to the current market as an accepted cost of trading a large number of shares.

Boiler room Derogatory term to describe a brokerage firm where investors are aggressively solicited over the telephone with high-pressure telephone sales tactics. Smug traders, stay well clear.

Bounce What happens to mail which for some reason (e.g. wrong e-mail address) cannot be delivered.

Breadth Comparison of issues traded on a stock exchange on a given day to the total number of issues listed for trading. The broader a market move the more significant it is.

Break A sudden fall in price.

Breakout When the price moves out of its recent range. Sometimes signals further moves in the direction of the breakout.

Broker An individual who executes customers' orders.

Bucket shop Slang term for a disreputable brokerage firm that regularly engages in illegal practices, such as selling customers' stock at a higher than market price without disclosing the fact.

Bull(ish) An individual who believes prices will rise.

Bull market A market in which prices are rising.

Bull spread An option position where it is intended to profit from a rising market. Usually the position involves the purchase of a call at one strike price and the sale of a call at a higher strike price.

Buy in A person having to buy a security because of an inability to deliver the shares from a previous sale of said shares. Often associated with short sellers.

Call option (calls) The right, but not the obligation, existing only for a fixed period of time, to purchase a fixed quantity of stock at a fixed price.

Cash flow per share The trailing 12-month cash flow divided by the 12-month average shares outstanding. All other things being equal, a relatively high figure, growing steadily, is a sign of a growing and healthy company and may indicate a rising share price.

Churning Illegal practice by a broker to cause excessive transactions in a client's account to benefit the broker through increased transaction fees.

Clerk An employee of an exchange's member firm, who is registered to work on the exchange floor.

Closed When referring to a position this means one has made an equal and opposite trade to one already held and so has no more exposure to the market on that trade.

Co-mingling Illegal act of combining client assets with those of the brokerage to boost the fiduciary's financial standing.

Contrarian An individual who generally believes it is usually better not to do what the majority is doing, because the majority does not make money.

Cookie According to conspiracy theorists, a cookie is a small piece of software that is downloaded from a website to your computer's hard drive that tells the web master all your hidden and deepest secrets. According to everyone else, a cookie is a small piece of software that is downloaded from a website to your computer's hard drive that tells the web master your user name, password, viewing preference and one or two other things. It means you do not have to enter the same information over and over again.

Crossed market The highest bid is greater than the lowest offer due to buyer and seller imbalance. Usually only lasts a few seconds until the market 'sorts itself out'.

Current ratio The ratio of total current assets divided by the total current liabilities for the same period. A measure of financial strength. All other things being equal, a relatively high figure would indicate a healthy company.

Cyberspace William Gibson's name in his fantasy novel *Neuromancer* (William Gibson, 1994) to describe what is now known as the internet.

Daisy chain Creating the illusion of trading activity in a stock through collusion of a number of brokers. Yes, it is illegal.

Day trade(r) A position that is closed the same day it was opened.

Deep discount Often, internet brokers that charge commissions far less than full service or discount brokers; as cheap as you can get.

Delta The change of the options price for a change in the underlying price. A delta of 0.5 means a 10-point move in the underlying price causes a five-point move in the option.

Depreciation An accounting measure used to reduce the value of capital expenditure for the purposes of reclaiming tax.

Diversification Reducing risk by spreading investments among different investments. Not putting all your eggs in a few baskets.

Dividend ex-date This is the date from which a purchaser of the stock will not be entitled to receive the last announced dividend. Appropriately, when a stock goes ex-dividend its price falls by approximately the value of the dividend.

Dividend growth rate A measure of corporate growth. The annual positive change in dividend paid to stock-holders. All other things being equal, an increase should indicate a growing company and should be reflected in rising share price.

Dividend rate This is the total expected dividends for the forthcoming 12 months. It is usually the value of the most recent dividend figure multiplied by the number of times dividends are paid in a year, plus any extra dividend payments.

Dividend yield This is calculated by dividing the annual dividend by the current price and expressing the figure as a percentage.

Domain Part of a web or e-mail address. Separated from the rest of the address by dots.

Dotted quad A set of four numbers separated by dots that constitutes an internet address, e.g. 123.32.433.234.

Down tick A trade in a security that was executed at a lower price than the previous trade; same as 'minus tick'.

EPS Earnings per share. A measure of corporate growth. The value of corporate earning divided by the number of shares outstanding. All other things being equal, a growing figure reflects a healthy growing company and should be reflected in the share price.

European option An option that is only exercisable at expiry.

Exercise Where the holder of an option uses his right to buy or sell the underlying security. Also means to work out.

Expiry The date up to which a trader can exercise his option.

Flame An e-mail that is abusive or argumentative. Usually includes the words 'You are a …' somewhere in the message.

Flamefest The same as a flame orgy.

Flat (1) A market where the price of a stock and/or its volume have not changed significantly over a period of time; (2) to no longer hold a position in a particular security or account.

Floor broker A member who executes orders for clearing members.

Floor trader An individual who trades on the floor of an exchange either for himself or for a company.

Free speech An issue relating to the internet about which the US Congress spends inordinate quantities of time. Essentially, the concern is to give rights to those who would deny them to others, including those who granted them.

Freeriding Rapid buying and selling of a security by a broker without putting up funds for the purchase. Yup, it is illegal.

Front running Buying or selling securities ahead of a large order so as to benefit from the subsequent price move.

FTP (file transfer protocol) The protocol for sending files through the internet.

Fundamental analysis Forecasting prices by using economic or accounting data. For example, one might base a decision to buy a stock on its yield.

Futures A standardized contract for the future delivery of goods, at a pre-arranged date, location, price.

Gap Where a price opens and trades higher than its previous close.

Geek Also known as a net nerd. They were the kids everyone hated at school, who wore thick black-rimmed spectacles and were extremely uncool. They would also get sand kicked in their faces and were so unpopular no one would be seen dead with them – sometimes not even their parents. Now the sand has settled, and it has become clear that because they were unpopular they spent all their time studying, and can now be considered some of the wealthiest people on the planet, with the fastest, flashiest cars. They definitely had the last laugh.

Gross margin A measure of company profitability. The previous 12-month total revenue less cost of goods sold divided by the total revenue. All other things being equal, a decrease in gross margins could indicate troubled times ahead.

Hedge Protection against current or anticipated risk exposure, usually through the purchase of a derivative. For example, if you hold euros and fear that the price will decline in relation to the dollar you may go long dollar. You would then make some profit on your long position to offset your losses in holding euros.

Hit the bid When a seller places market orders with the intention of selling to the highest bidder, regardless of price.

Implied volatility Future price volatility as calculated from actual, not theoretical, options prices. The volatility is implied in the prices.

In and out Term for day trading in a security.

Income per employee The income after taxes divided by the number of employees. A measure of corporate efficiency. All other things being equal, the greater the figure, or a growing figure, indicates a more efficient company and should be reflected in a rising share price.

Initial margin requirement Amount of cash and securities a customer must have in his/her account before trading on margin.

Initial public offering (IPO) First sale of stock by a company to the public.

Insider Person such as a corporate officer or director with access to privileged company information.

Insider share purchases The number of shares in the company purchased by its insiders – officers and directors – over a stated period of time. All other things being equal, a relatively large move may indicate a forthcoming upward move in the stock price.

INSTINET A 'fourth stock market' allowing members to display bid and ask quotes and bypass brokers in securities transactions. Owned by Reuters.

Institutional net shares purchased This is the difference between institutional share purchases less institutional share sales in the company over a stated period of time. All other things being equal, a relatively large move may indicate a forthcoming upward move in the stock price.

Institutional per cent owned This is the percentage of shares owned by all the institutions taken together. It is a percentage of the total shares outstanding. All other things being equal, a relatively large move may indicate a forthcoming upward move in the stock price.

Intranet This is a collection of computers connected to one another and usually located in a company or other organization. Unlike the internet, the network is private and not principally intended for the public.

Java An island or a coffee bean or a programming language developed by Sun Microsystems. It allows users to do lots of clever things with web pages.

LAN (local area network) A network of computers operating up to a few thousand meters from each other.

Level I quotes Basic service of the Nasdaq stock market that displays current bid and ask quotes.

Level II quotes Service of the Nasdaq stock market that displays current bid and ask quotes and the bids and asks from all market makers in a particular stock.

Level III quotes Service of the Nasdaq stock market that allows a market maker or registered broker–dealer to enter a bid or ask on the electronic trading system.

Limit The maximum permitted price-move up or down for any given day, under exchange rules.

Liquid market A market which permits relatively easy entry and exit of large orders because there are so many buyers and sellers. Usually a characteristic of a popular market.

Long A position, opened but not yet closed, with a buy order.

Long-term debt to total equity A measure of financial strength. The long-term debt of the company divided by the total shareholder equity for the same period. All other things being equal, a relatively high figure may indicate an unhealthy company.

Margin A sum placed with a broker by a trader to cover against possible losses.

Margin call A demand for cash to maintain margin requirements.

Mark to market Daily calculation of paper gains and losses using closing market prices. Also used to calculate any necessary margin that may be payable.

Market capitalization This is the product of the number of shares outstanding and the current price.

Market order See At the market.

MIME Multi-purpose internet mail extensions. This enables you to attach files to e-mail.

Momentum An indicator used by traders to buy or sell. It is based on the theory that the faster and further prices move in a particular direction, the more likely they are to slow and turn.

Moving average A system used by traders to determine when to buy and sell. An average (simple, exponential, or other) is taken of the closing (or opening, or other) prices over a specific number of previous days. A plot is made based on the average. As each day progresses, the moving average has to be recalculated to take account of the latest data and remove the oldest data.

Net After expenses, or short for the internet.

Net profit margin A measure of profitability. Income after taxes divided by the total revenue for the same period.

All other things being equal, downward pressure on the net profit margin could provide advance warning of impending share price decline.

Netiquette Proper net behaviour. For instance, swearing is neither appropriate etiquette nor is it netiquette.

Network A group of computers connected to each other so that their users can access each others' machines.

Offer A price at which a seller is willing to sell.

Off-line browser A browser that permits viewing of sites previously downloaded without being connected to the net.

Open position A position that has not yet been closed and therefore the trader is exposed to market movements.

Overbought/oversold A term used to mean, broadly, that a stock is likely not to advance further and may decline (overbought) or advance (oversold).

Position Trades which result in exposure to market movements.

Price, 52-week high This is the highest price the stock traded in the last 52 weeks. It may not necessarily be a closing high, it could be an intra-day high.

Price, 52-week low This is the lowest price the stock traded in the past 52 weeks. Could be an intra-day low price.

Price to book ratio The current price divided by the latest quarterly book value per share. All other things being equal, a relatively low figure may indicate the stock is undervalued.

Price to cash flow ratio The current price divided by the cash flow per share for the trailing 12 months. All other things being equal, a relatively low figure may indicate the stock is undervalued.

Price to earnings ratio The current share price divided by earnings per share before extraordinary items, usually taken over the previous 12 months. All other things being equal, a relatively low figure may indicate the stock is undervalued.

Protocols A set of rules with which two computers must comply in order to communicate.

Push technology The internet can be quite a passive experience, needing the user to log on to a site to determine if changes have occurred, or to download information. With push technology, the browser can be set to download data automatically from a set site.

Put option A right, but not the obligation, existing for a specified period of time, to sell a specific quantity of stock or other instrument at a specified price.

Pyramiding The increase in size of an existing position by opening further positions, usually in decreasing increments.

Quick ratio A measure of financial strength. Cash plus short-term investments plus accounts receivable divided by current liabilities for the same period. All other things being equal, a relatively high figure may indicate a healthy company. See also Acid test ratio.

Return on assets A measure of management effectiveness. Income after taxes divided by the total assets. All other things being equal, a relatively high or growing figure may indicate a company doing well.

Return on equity A measure of management effectiveness. Income available to shareholders divided by the total common equity. All other things being equal, a relatively high or growing figure may indicate a company doing well.

Return on investments A measure of management effectiveness. Income after taxes divided by the average total assets and long-term debt. All other things being equal, a relatively high or growing figure may indicate a company doing well.

Revenue per cent change year on year A measure of growth. The revenue of the most recent period less the revenue of the previous period divided by the revenue of the previous period. All other things being equal, a growing figure indicates a growing company and should be reflected in a rising share price.

Sales change (as a percentage) A measure of corporate growth. The value of sales for the current period less the value of sales for the preceding period divided by the value of sales for the preceding period, expressed as a percentage. All other things being equal, a growing figure indicates a growing company and should be reflected in a rising share price.

Sales per employee A measure of company efficiency. The total sales divided by the total number of full-time employees. All other things being equal, the greater this figure the more efficient the company.

Scalper A trader who seeks to enter and exit the market very quickly and thereby make a lot of small profits.

Seat Exchange membership that permits floor trading.

Server A computer that shares its resources with others. The resources may be disk space, or files, or something else.

Shares outstanding The number of shares issued less those held in treasury.

Short An open position created by a sell order, in the expectation of a price decline and so the opportunity to profit by purchasing the instrument (so 'closing out') at a lower price.

Short-term debt The value of debt due in the next 12 months.

SMTP (simple mail transfer protocol) The standard set of rules for transferring e-mail messages from one computer to another.

Speculator An individual who purchases financial instruments in order to profit. Often used to refer to a non-professional. Sometimes used derogatorily.

Spread The simultaneous purchase of one contract and the sale of a similar, but not identical, contract. Depending on the exact combination, a profit can be made from either a rising or falling market.

Stop order (stop-loss orders) An order left with a broker instructing him to close out an existing position if the market price reaches a certain level. Can be used to take profits or stop losses.

TCP/IP (transmission control protocol/internet protocol) A set of rules used to connect to other computers.

Technical analysis Method used to forecast future prices using the price data alone (for example, by plotting them on a chart and noting direction) or using the price as an input in mathematical formulae and plotting the results. See also Fundamental analysis.

Technical rally or decline A price movement resulting from factors unrelated to fundamentals or supply and demand.

Tick The smallest possible price move.

Total debt to equity ratio A measure of financial strength. The total debt divided by total shareholder equity for the same period. All other things being equal, a relatively low figure is a sign of a healthy company.

Total operating expenses A measure of the cost of running the company. All other things being equal, a lower figure is preferable to a higher one.

Trendline A line on a price chart indicating market price direction. The line connects at least three price points which touch the line, with no prices breaking the line.

Volatility A statistical indication of probable future price movement size (but not direction) within a period of time. For example 66 per cent probability of a 15 pence move in three months.

Webcasting This is the internet trying to be older – like TV or radio. Instead of viewing pages, you view a stream of data in the form of radio or video. Unfortunately, the infrastructure is lacking to make this a popular alternative to TV and radio.

Whipsaw A price move first in one direction, and, shortly thereafter, in another direction thereby catching traders wrong-footed. Such markets may be termed 'choppy'. Such effects often give rise to false buy and sell signals, leading to losses.

Further reading

H Abell, **The Day Trader's Advantage**, Dearborn Financial 1996. A little dated from the ubiquitous Abell, who seems to be a full-time author producing what feels like one book per month. Focuses on the trading psychology aspects of day trading.

Carroll Aby, **Point and Figure Charting**, Traders Press 1996. Both a beginners' guide and a reference book for this method of plotting prices.

Steven B Achelis, **Technical Analysis from A to Z**, Probus 1995. A good introductory guide which is comprehensive. Lots of pics of indicators.

Gerald Appel, **The Moving Average Convergence-Divergence Method**, Signalert 1979. Appel is the creator of this highly popular trading method, and this book explains it straight from the source's mouth. Useful if you plan to place large weight on this indicator in your own trading.

Gerald Appel and Fred Hitschler, **Stock Market Trading Systems**, Dow Jones Irwin 1980. This is a classic and discusses the price ROC and moving average trading systems among others. It is always best to go to the original source to gain insights which later secondary texts are likely to miss.

Richard Arms, **Volume Cycles in the Stock Market**, Equis 1994. Arms is a well-known technical analyst and this book delves in depth into volume. If volume analysis is something you intend using then this a very good source of information.

Robert Barnes, **High Impact Day Trading**, Irwin 1996. This book highlights the author's Mountain Valley system, going for longer moves and ignoring shorter ones. It has proved a very popular title.

J Bernstein, **The Compleat Day Trader**, McGraw-Hill 1999. A very good seller, with an unusual title. Covers not only day trading but also risk management.

The Bhagavad Gita, **Trading psychology**. Various editions. Although written more than 2,000 years ago, and not directly about trading, I found it to be one of the most useful 'trading' books I have ever read. It largely discusses discipline – how and why – and the benefits of discipline. Since a lack of mental discipline is one of the major downfalls of traders, this is likely to be a very profitable read.

William Blau, **Momentum Direction and Divergence**, Wiley 1995. Definitely for the advanced user. If, after learning about oscillators, you want to take things further and uncover some mathematics to better understand their weaknesses then this is a good book.

Philip L Carret, **The Art of Speculation**, Wiley 1997. Apparently highly regarded by Victor Nieder-hoffer. However, in spite of that, I would recommend it as a good read.

AW Cohen, **How to Use the Three-Point Reversal Method of Point and Figure Stock Market Trading**, Chartcraft 1984. Despite the cumbersome title this is a useful book on this popular method of drawing charts.

R Colby and T Meyers, **Encyclopedia of Technical Market Indicators**, Business One Irwin 1988. As one would expect of a book claiming to be an encyclopedia this is an exhaustive study. It will be most useful if you want a good overview before settling down on a few chosen indicators.

John Cox and Mark Rubinstein, **The Options Markets**, Prentice Hall 1985. This is a classic text on options. The book is about valuing options – these authors, of course, created the famous Cox–Rubinstein option pricing model.

Robert Daigler, **Advanced Options Trading**, Probus 1993. This book moves beyond basics and discusses some strategies generally used only by the professionals. That does not mean a private investor using them will have hit upon some sector – so beware. But if you are interested in knowing more than just the basics, this book is better than most.

David DeRosa, **Options on Foreign Exchanges**, Probus 1992. Not to leave out the currency-option boys and girls, this market specialist covers valuation of options and pricing of currencies, as well as how the various markets work. Probably useful for the beginner and intermediate-level trader in forex options.

Edward Dobson, **Understanding Fibonacci Numbers**, Traders Press 1984. Not too difficult to understand if Fibonacci fascinates.

Mark Douglas, **The Disciplined Trader**, Prentice Hall 1990. An extremely good book. Written in a very intelligent fashion and gets away from 'Mickey Mouse'-fashion psychology. Deserves a far higher profile than it has to date received.

S Eckett, **Investing Online**, FT Pitman 1997. Encyclopaedic in coverage and an excellent reference tool with a focus on global investing.

William Eng, **Trading Rules**, FT Pitman 1995. While some of the rules will be familiar, others provide valuable enough information to justify buying this easy-to-understand book.

C Farrell, **Day Trade Online**, Wiley 1999. Farrell is a young man who trades for a living. Some good content in here, but lay-out, design and substance lacking in other respects.

Robert Fischer, **Fibonacci Applications and Strategies for Traders**, Wiley 1993. Take Fibonacci study further with this book. While you do not necessarily need such detailed knowledge, if you are going to use it, you may as well know all there is.

Kenneth Fisher, **100 Minds that Made the Market**, Business Classics 1991. Biographical in nature and the profiles are somewhat short, but nevertheless a good bedtime or holiday read.

M Friedfertig and G West, **Electronic Day Traders' Secrets**, McGraw-Hill 1999. This book has a series of interviews with day traders from Friedfertig's own brokerage company. A lot of trading psychology here, but light on strategies.

D Gerlach, **The Complete Idiot's Guide to Online Investing**, Que 1999. Que are known for their computer books and this venture appears to be a bandwagon thing. But the Complete Idiot's guides can be clear and more comprehensible if you are, um, well, a complete idiot.

Elli Gifford, **The Investor's Guide to Technical Analysis**, FT Pitman 1995. While the book uses UK companies to illustrate points, it is nevertheless useful to traders in any country. Thorough, comprehensive, and easy to read and understand. Good as a starter and for more advanced study; however, it is not mathematical.

William Grandmill, **Soybean Trading and Hedging, Wheat Trading and Hedging, Corn Trading and Hedging, Investing in Wheat, Soybeans, Corn,**

Irwin Professional 1988, 1989, 1990, 1991 (respectively). A series of books by the appropriately named Grandmill for commodity traders. Grandmill provides details of the commodities, and his own systems for picking entry and exit points. If you think it is best to become an expert in one area of commodity trading then books such as these should be a good starting point to developing your skills and understanding.

William Grandmill, **Make Money with S&P Options**, **How to Make Money with Corn Options**, **Make Money with Soybean Options**, Irwin 1989, 1990, 1990 (respectively). If you are concentrating on one of these areas and feeling you need something specifically addressing your trading needs, then these books were written with you in mind. Grandmill is a prolific writer and knows what he is talking about.

Joseph Granville, **New Strategy of Daily Stock Market Timing for Maximum Profit**, Prentice Hall 1976. Another one of the technical analysis gods. This book discusses on-balance volume in particular. Granville created that indicator, so who better to learn more about it from?

Alvin D Hall, **Getting Started in Stocks**, Wiley 1997 (3rd edition). A very good primer for stocks. Hall has a clear style and injects humour now and again to alleviate the rigour.

Charles Kindleberger, **Manias, Panics and Crashes**, Wiley 1996. Why do the economists, statisticians and government nerds always get it wrong? This book does not provide any answers, but it does provide some insights.

George Kleinman, **Mastering Commodity Futures and Options**, FT Pitman 1997. This book is very well-presented indeed. A little like a textbook in style, but covers the ground very well for both beginner and intermediate user.

Knight-Ridder, **The CRB Commodity Yearbook**, Knight-Ridder annual. A very useful reference guide to commodities. Filled with data, charts, tables and articles on trends and strategies. If you are serious about commodities you should have this.

Robert Koppel and Howard Abell, **The Inner Game of Trading**, Irwin Professional 1997. Includes interviews with some leading traders, but its value comes from the analysis of psychological difficulties traders are likely to encounter. Definitely recommended.

John Labuszewski, **Trading Options on Futures**, Wiley 1998. This covers treasuries, currencies and commodities. I think if you are trading options on futures there is more to it than understanding options and understanding futures. The whole is greater than the sum of the parts, and therefore a book such as this is added value in being exclusively written for one trading sector.

Edwin Le Fevre, **Reminiscences of a Stock Operator**, Wiley 1994 (reprint edition). An undoubted classic. The fictionalized trading biography of Jesse Livermore, one of the greatest speculators ever seen. While dated (it was written in 1923), it nevertheless provides some insight into the difficulties encountered by traders. A very enjoyable read.

Todd Lofton, **Getting Started in Futures**, Wiley 1997 (3rd edition). Very clear and easy to understand as well as giving lots of information for delving deeper.

Charles Mackay and Joseph de la Vega, **Extraordinary Popular Delusions and the Madness of Crowds and Confusion de Confusiones**, Wiley 1995. Explores crowd psychology and how that affects market movement. While its examinations are 300 years old, it is highly relevant today. Short and interesting.

Lawrence McMillan, **McMillan on Options**, Wiley 1996. Brands itself as the 'Bible' of the options markets. Why do publishers refer to their books as the 'Bible' of something? I wonder if they mean only a minority of people will ever read the book but more are supposed to and it competes with equivalent books for the rest. Anyway, that aside, McMillan goes beyond explaining the basics about options and actually applies a degree of critique. Should consider if you are a beginner.

John Murphy, **The Visual Investor**, Wiley 1996. Former CNBC presenter provides a good primer on technical analysis. He draws on one of the key aspects of technical analysis – it is visual.

David S Nassar, **How to Get Started in Electronic Day Trading**, McGraw-Hill 1999. Nassar owns a day-trading firm, and this book is written from the perspective of a man who knows his business.

David S Nassar, **The 22 Rules of Day Trading Online**, McGraw-Hill 1999. After the success of his earlier day-trading book, David Nassar returns with a different format.

Sheldon Natenberg, **Option Volatility & Pricing Strategies**, Probus 1994. Natenberg is a leader in this field. This book is definitely for the more advanced trader wanting to dig into option mechanics.

Steven Nison, **Japanese Candlestick Charting Techniques**, New York Institute of Finance 1991. Steve Nison is regarded as the expert on Japanese candlesticks. This book is very clear and very easy to understand. Nison uses actual charts and not stylized fictional ones. He also focuses on how and when the chart indications fail. The book helps an understanding of the rationale behind technical analysis, why it works, and why it does not. Excellent.

Grant Noble, **The Trader's Edge**, Probus 1995. Some very useful insights into what they do on the floor. A good insider's view and useful pointers on some of the advantages.

Alpesh B Patel, **Trading Online**, FT Prentice Hall 2000. New and revised version of the best-seller covering all the steps to trading from getting set up to monitoring positions.

Alpesh B Patel, **The Mind of a Trader**, FT Pitman 1997. Advice on becoming a better trader from the world's leading traders, including Pat Arbor, former Chairman of the Chicago Board of Trade, and Bill Lipschutz, former Global Head of Forex at Salomon Brothers, who made on average $250,000 each and every trading day he was there, for eight years!

Martin Pring, **Technical analysis, Technical Analysis Explained**, McGraw-Hill 1991. The first half of this book is more relevant than the second. While a little disappointing, nevertheless provides insights not available elsewhere.

Martin Pring, **Martin Pring on Market Momentum**, McGraw-Hill 1993. Aimed at the user who has chosen momentum as one technical indicator from his arsenal and wants to learn more, this book is typical Pring; clear and useful. Unfortunately Pring maintains his habit of stylized artificial charts instead of giving more real market illustrations to make his points.

Alan Rubenfeld, **The Super Traders**, Irwin 1992. Nine profiles of traders from diverse backgrounds. While a little bit too biographical, nevertheless makes for a good read.

Jack Schwager, **A Complete Guide to the Futures**

Markets, Wiley 1984. This book covers fundamental analysis and technical analysis as well as spreads and options. Characteristic of Schwager's books, it is very thorough.

Jack Schwager, **Market Wizards**, **New Market Wizards**, Harper Business 1993, Wiley 1995 (respectively). An absolute must. Fascinating, although since it's in a question and answer format you are left to draw many of your own conclusions.

Kenneth Shaleen, **Volume and Open Interest**, Irwin 1996. A good starter to investigating these two popular statistics in technical analysis. Probably unavoidable if you are trading futures.

Larry Spears, **Commodity Options,** Marketplace Books 1985. This one is for beginners who may not have settled on a particular commodity and want an overview.

Peter Temple, **Traded Options**, 3rd edn, Pearson Education 2001. For those trading options on LIFFE. Thorough and explains all the basics, from what options are to buying software.

Michael Thomsett, **Getting Started in Options**, Wiley 1993. Again, very clear and easy to understand. An excellent start for beginners.

Russell Wasendorf and Thomas McCafferty, **All About Options**, Probus 1993. The good thing about this book is that it covers both strategies and some of the background mechanics behind options, such as what happens on the trading floor.

Neal Weintraub, **Tricks of the Floor Trader**, Irwin 1996. One of the few books of its kind. Gives the outsider a view of what the insider does. Provides knowledge which is useful to know.

Welles J Wilder, **New Concepts in Technical Trading Systems**, Trend Research 1978. Wilder is very highly regarded in the technical analysis world. Here he explains and interprets numerous indicators, including RSI.

L Williams, **Long-term Secrets to Short-term Trading**, Wiley 1999. Larry Williams is a proven trader. An excellent book, because he clearly knows his stuff and trades off it.

M Anthony Wong, **Trading and Investing in Bond Options**, Wiley 1991. This title covers strategies and pricing models and details the peculiarities of trading this market using options.

Martin Zweig, **Winning on Wall Street**, Warner Books 1997 (revised edition). Zweig is famous for his market reports and for being one of Schwager's market wizards. I found a copy of this book for $11.99 – you can't go wrong.

Index